# Testimonials

"*Rounding Home* is a raw and honest view of the struggles and challenges of a family learning to deal with the life-changing realities of having a child diagnosed with special needs. Those stresses profoundly affect all those who care for and love that child, as well as the child him- or herself. This story of the Swindell family is a poignant demonstration of how each family member responded and was changed, for better or worse, as they struggled to come to terms with how their lives had been altered. And although there was damage along the way, they ultimately triumph by rekindling the love that created their family unit in the first place."

—DR. BRYAN JEPSON, AUTHOR, PHYSICIAN, AND
FATHER OF TWO SONS WITH AUTISM

\* \* \* \* \* \*

"As a professional, friend and mother of an adult son with profound autism, I am honored to know Sarah, the strong woman behind the voice that wrote this thoroughly interesting, poignant and eloquent account of her life. She gives voice to not only her experience(s) with her son with Autism, but how that had, and still has, profound effects on the entire family system, and all webbed in relationship with them. She skillfully weaves in her 'wise adult' insights, which adds richness and feeling to the reader's experience."

—DR. DOROTHY BYRNE, PHD, LPC-S, CHT, RDN, LD, AUTISM MOM

\* \* \* \* \* \*

"In *Rounding Home*, Sarah writes with gritty honesty, a deeply moving account of life with her autistic son. However, this is more than another autism book. It is the gripping story of the Swindell family over the course of many very tumultuous years. Sarah shares vulnerability, passion, and true love for her family. This testament to the resilience of the human spirit will touch your heart and soul."

—GAYLE NOBEL, LIFE COACH, AUTISM MOM, AND
AUTHOR OF THREE BOOKS ON LIVING WITH AUTISM

\* \* \* \* \* \*

"*Rounding Home* is a gorgeously transparent and inspiring chronicle of The Swindell Family. This astonishing memoir speaks to anyone who yearns for deeper, truer relationships and a more abundant, authentic life."

—KELLY TAYLOR-SIMMONS, AUTISM MOM TO 14-YEAR-OLD, PIERCE

\* \* \* \* \* \*

"*Rounding Home* is not at all what you'd expect. Instead, Sarah grabs and takes you through her roller coaster of life as a mother of four (one with special needs), baseball wife, infidelity, several marriages and divorces, heartache, loneliness, laughter and brings us back to what started this roller coaster journey—that one true love! Sarah shares it all with us, with honesty and grace."

—JOANIE FRIEDEN, AUSTIN BUSINESS OWNER

\* \* \* \* \* \*

"*Rounding Home* is a riveting, page-turning masterpiece chronicling the sometimes heartbreaking, and always resilient Sarah, and how she and her family overcame adversity. The sheer vulnerability and grit demonstrated by Sarah is inspirational and unforgettable."

—ERICA MANTEI, FORMER BASEBALL WIFE

\* \* \* \* \* \*

"*Rounding Home* takes you on a riveting journey through the eyes of an exceptional woman who embraced struggle, love, success and the unimaginable, Autism. You weave through Sarah's brave journey to home base through her strength, unconditional love, profound forgiveness, and perseverance. Get ready to laugh, cry and flutter with romance, it's one hell of a love story!"

—GENA LEE NOLIN, ACTRESS, AUTHOR, ADVOCATE—
"THYROID SEXY," WIFE & MOTHER

# Rounding Home

A Memoir of Love, Betrayal, Heartbreak, and Hope
with an Intimate Look into Raising a Child with Severe Autism

To Chrissie!

# SARAH SWINDELL

For information about this title or to order other books and/or electronic media, contact the publisher:
Sarah Swindell
Sarah@roundinghome.net

ISBN:  978-17330277-0-0 (Softcover)
       978-1-7330277-2-4 (Hardcover)
       978-17330277-1-7 (eBook)

Printed in the United States of America

Cover and Interior design: 1106 Design
Cover photo: Nicolai McCrary Photography
Author photo: Brenna Wommack

*For Zeke and our beautiful children, the OG.*
*Randee, Denise, Cynthia and Sue, my forever friends.*
*Most of all, for those affected by autism, and the*
*families and caregivers who love them.*

# Disclaimers

This book is a memoir. It reflects the author's present recollections of experiences over time. I have tried to recreate events, locales, and conversations from my memories of them and to the best of my ability. Some names and characteristics have been changed, some events have been compressed, and some dialogue has been recreated for storytelling purposes. Some dates and events may not be in the exact order that they occurred. My opinions in this book are not meant to replace professional medical advice from a pediatrician and/or primary care physician. The author shall not be liable or responsible for any loss or damage allegedly arising from any information or suggestions in this book.

### *Hotlines in the U.S.*
*All hotlines listed below are free and confidential.*

### National Suicide Prevention Lifeline
**800-273-TALK (8255)**
The National Suicide Prevention Lifeline is open 24 hours a day, every day. Services are also available for veterans and for Spanish speakers.

### The Trevor Project
**866-488-7386** – a hotline for LGBT youth

### Autism Society of America
www.autism.org
1-800-328-8467

# Foreword

THIS STORY IS FOR ALL the women out there who have ever felt lost, broken, scared, betrayed, or felt as if they could not go on one more day in the life they were living. Being a parent is hard, being a wife is hard, and watching your child suffer is the hardest of all. We have all had, or will have, traumatic experiences and painful moments, no matter how hard we try to avoid them. It's the choices we make during those moments that can change everything.

My hope in telling my own story is that you find comfort. That you understand that you are not alone and that you may learn from the mistakes I made. Never forget that love, in various ways, is right in front of you, waiting to give you comfort. You have to dig deep and find the courage to go toward it, embrace it and forgive yourself and others when you stumble along the way.

I stumbled too many times to count over the years. Trust me, I have questioned my own sanity many times while writing this story. Some may not get it at all, and some may breathe a huge sigh of relief knowing they are not alone in their struggles. I realize that while some events were out of my control, I also realize I made situations even worse by my own accord. Because of that, I also have learned the valuable lesson of forgiveness and grace for myself and for others.

I have done my best to keep the timeline of events as accurate as possible, but I may be off in places by a few months and quite possibly even a year or two. I have changed a few names, physical characteristics, locations, and selectively left out events that might cause harm to others, most of all to my husband and children. While some of the events I talk about might be difficult to read or cause pain for some involved, my thoughts and feelings about those events are important in painting the whole picture. If this is the case, I am truly sorry, and it was not my intention.

This story is about my own journey through a challenging period in my life. I did my best to keep it authentic as to what I was feeling, while still being truthful, in as much detail as I felt necessary and to the best of my recollection. While this book has been professionally edited, I have asked them to keep it as close to my voice as possible. I am far from a writer, but have always felt I have a story to tell. Some of the conversations in the book have been created to give the reader an idea of my characters' personalities and a general idea of real conversations that took place.

# Acknowledgments

To My One True Love. Zeke, I thank you for the text you sent me when I was making tater-tot casserole. You literally had me at hello from the moment I opened that door in 1992. You are the one I want to sit in a recliner holding hands with as we drink boxed wine for the rest of my life. This is our beautiful and messy love story, and I thank you for allowing me to share it, even the very difficult parts. You are my everything and I love you "fo real doe."

To my beautiful daughters, Hayley, Brenna, and Sophia. Your support and encouragement to share this story gives me more strength than you will ever know. Thank you for always standing by me, even when I sometimes didn't deserve it. Most of all, thank you for being the most amazing sisters to your little brother; he hit the jackpot with you three! I am so incredibly blessed to be your mom and proud of you in too many ways to count. You fill my soul, and I love you all with all my heart.

To my sweet boy, Dawson. You have changed me for the better, and you are my reason for everything good in my life, even when I wasn't always aware of it. Without saying a single word, you have shown me the true meaning of love, and your strength in all that you have endured is nothing short of heroic. There is not one person that has met you and NOT fallen in love. I love you more than you love french fries!

My amazing parents, you have always been on my side and truly gave me the best life I could have wished for. Most of all, thank you for being a real example of what a marriage should look like. Your love for each other is a gift you have given to all of your children, grandchildren, and grandchildren to come; it is still beautiful to watch. You both embody what loving and devoted parents should be. I wish you would write a guidebook for the world to follow. I love you, Mom and Dad!

To my brothers who make me laugh harder than anyone else in the world and who continued to love me through all of my bad choices, thank you. Mel, you are like as sister to me and I love you, even during our "tough love" talks, because that's what sisters do. Beth, my real sister, you are the strongest woman I know, and Justine was so lucky to have you as her mommy. I know she would have LOVED to read this book and would have been my biggest cheerleader. I love you both!

For the entire Swindell family, I can't thank you enough for welcoming me in your lives, both times, and for loving me, no matter how messy things got. To Greg's mom Tonii, you are an amazing mother and now great-great-grandmother; we are so blessed to have you in our lives! Chrystie Swindell, you are an angel in every way possible.

To the many teachers, therapists, nurses and doctors who have helped Dawson throughout his life. Without you, we would have been lost. The love and concern you have shown not only to him but to me and my family will never be forgotten.

A very special thank you to these people who have made a tremendous impact on my life in various and beautiful ways; the Bravo Family, Southwest Autism Research and Resource Center, Reach Unlimited, Justine Varga, Karie Dozer, Jennifer Thompson, Beverly Owen, Aaron Blocher-Rubin, Gayle Nobel, Jennifer Wright, Lexie Mader, Angie Balmer, Dorothy Byrne, Julie Pierce, Kacie Hall, Christy May, Kelly

# Acknowledgments

Taylor-Simmons, Dr. Andrew Wakefield, Dr. Arthur Krigsman, Dell Children's Hospital, Texas Children's Hospital, the Blue Bird Clinic in Houston, TX, Dr. Jay Shapiro and his nursing staff, all the beautiful baseball wives that were family for so many years, and Major League Baseball for allowing my husband to live his dream and for giving me and my children the chance to watch it all happen. It all still feels like a dream!

For my Austin girlfriends, you know who you all are, and I am truly blessed to have you in my life. You all are the strongest and most beautiful women I know. Laughing (and sometimes crying) with you is you is my favorite past time!

To my incredibly patient editors, Sue Gallup, Cecily Sailer, and especially to my dear friend Sue White. Boy, did you all have your work cut out! Your encouragement, suggestions, and ability to not laugh at all my errors is pretty amazing. Each of you understood my desire to keep this story in my real voice, even though it probably didn't sound correct all the time. There is no way I could have done this without you, and I know it wasn't easy. Thank you from the bottom of my heart.

And last but not least, this is for all the children and adults affected by autism or any other disability. To the parents, siblings, and caregivers who get up each and every day to a world that is sometimes frightening to face, but do it anyway with hope and pure love in their hearts. It's not easy and never will be. You all are heroes in a million different ways and inspiration in millions more.

# Prologue
## *Austin, Texas – Winter 2011*

I HAVE EXPERIENCED SADNESS before, but it was nothing compared to the incredible hopelessness, exhaustion and fear I felt in those early morning hours. I wondered, was the exhaustion from lack of sleep, or was I simply tired of this life? My mind was as foggy as the weather outside, and the depression I felt was as heavy as a cloak I just could not seem to take off, no matter how hard I tried.

There is nothing easy about having a severely autistic child. At ten years old, Dawson was in one of the most difficult phases in his young life. At the same time, I was undoubtedly in the most difficult phase of my own life, and that certainly didn't make our situation any better. Dawson hardly ever slept, and it seemed that for the last ten years, I was constantly in the "new mommy" phase, continually sleep deprived. I always felt like I just needed to lie down for a minute and shut my eyes.

Dawson makes these loud vocal noises; in the autism world they are called *verbal stims*. *Verbal stims* are essentially a coping mechanism autistic children form to help ease the stress they are experiencing, or to drown out things around them that are intolerable. It wasn't too bad during the day, but in the middle of the night, those sounds became almost unbearable and certainly impossible to sleep through.

Sometimes he would cry in the night as if he was in immense pain, but because Dawson is nonverbal, he was never able to tell me what was wrong or show me where it hurt. It was a constant guessing game for me to understand how to help ease his pain and what to do next. Despite all of the intensive therapy we were doing, he just wasn't making the progress I had desperately hoped for so many years ago. My heart ached for my son, he had to live such a confusing and too-often painful life. To love a child as much as I love Dawson, and to have no idea how to help him, is impossible to describe. At times, I was literally paralyzed with fear just thinking about his future; and now, on top of all of that, I was scared for my own.

It was the third time that week I had to get Dawson out of the house in the middle of the night so my teenage daughters could get the rest they needed for school. Those destinationless drives would take me all around Austin as the rest of the city slept. I was so exhausted, tears started to pool in my tired, burning eyes as I strapped Dawson into the back seat and grabbed my coffee off the hood of the car. He started to fuss a little, so I gave him his bowl of Chex to snack on and his beloved silk ribbon that in a way was his security blanket and usually would keep him occupied for a while. I didn't bother to put on my shoes or a bra, as I slipped into the driver's seat looking more than a bit disheveled.

I backed out of the driveway and pushed my Dixie Chicks CD in. I knew that I was only torturing myself by listening to it when I was already so upset, but I did it anyway. This was our music, Greg's and mine.

As the Dixie Chicks sang, my mind raced back to all that had happened in the last year and a half. Tears started to pour down my face as a profound sadness filled my entire body. Even though Greg's affair with my best friend had happened over a year ago, the heartbreaking images of them together were etched in my brain. It played over and over and over like a horror movie that I was being forced to sit and watch. I was still filled with so many questions and no real answers.

I missed Greg so much it hurt, while at the same time I hated him for what he had done to me and to our family. But I hated her more; she plotted, planned and pretended to be my best friend as she intentionally stole my husband and shattered my family into a million pieces.

How was I going to continue living this way? I was so tired in every way possible, I felt as if life was dragging me down a path I didn't have the strength to endure any longer. I felt like a failure as a mother; not only was I unable to help my son who was so clearly struggling, I wasn't present for my three daughters who desperately needed me, as well. My life had once been a beautiful fairy tale and now it felt like an ugly living nightmare, and I was terrified to continue living in it. My dark, clouded mind whispered that my children would be better off without me, a new stepmother down the road would most certainly do a better job than I ever could; at least she would be a better example for my daughters. I loved Dawson so much, I just couldn't figure out how to cope with his daily struggles through life anymore. I wondered if he was as miserable as I was. How could he not be?

I sped up as I approached the overpass. It was still dark out, the only illumination detectable emanated from the dim lights of empty stores in the distance, fuzzy through the thick layer of fog still blanketing the city. There were hardly any cars on the road this early in the morning, and I wondered if anyone would even notice when we sailed through the concrete barrier.

Would my car crashing to the pavement below make a sound loud enough for anyone to hear? Was the overpass high enough? Was I going fast enough? I sped up a little more as I gripped the wheel a little tighter.

Few people think they had the perfect childhood, but I do. This makes the events in my life so hard for me to explain. While I can't blame myself for all of it, I do blame myself for a lot of it. I blame myself for how sideways things became for me, and more importantly, for my children. I realize the word "perfect" means different things to different people, but when describing my childhood, it's the only word I come back to over and over again.

I was the youngest of four children, and my siblings would probably agree that I was a bit spoiled since I was the last. Growing up I had a large group of close friends, rode my beloved green Schwinn ten-speed bike everywhere in my neighborhood, and had summers filled with sleepovers and summer camps. We ate dinner as a family together almost every single night, and laughter was always present at our table. On the rare occasion when my mother didn't cook, we would all pile into my dad's Cadillac and drive to Champions Country Club for dinner. This was always my favorite thing to do. I loved the tinkling piano, fragrant flowers, and the little baskets of crackers with pats of butter wrapped in gold paper. I could never get enough of them. I even loved the tiny bowl of pastel mints in the beautifully decorated ladies room, with a gold-plated sink and plush pink carpet.

My mother always looked beautiful. She was equally as beautiful dressed up for a night out, as she was in the terry cloth zip-up bathrobe she wore every morning. She had an unpretentious elegant style and grace about her. She was tall and thin with just the right amount of curl in her naturally blonde hair; she always looked as if she had just stepped out of the salon. Her perfume was this soft floral scent which I called "the mommy smell." My own children would also call it the mommy smell as they were growing up.

Most of all, she was kind, loving, and always there for us. She would draw funny little faces with colorful markers on the hard-boiled eggs she put in my lunch every day and wrote sweet notes of encouragement on my napkins. She taught Sunday School when we were little, volunteered at the hospital, and was home to greet us with her big, loving smile and a hug every day after school. She definitely gave June Cleaver a run for her money, and I wanted nothing more than to be just like her when I grew up.

My father was just as handsome as my mother was beautiful. He was smart, witty, and was always the life of the party. He was the president of a small oil company and worked hard to give us what we wanted, but without spoiling us. He did, however, enjoyed spoiling my mom. Every Christmas there would be a tiny, beautifully wrapped box under the tree for her holding a gorgeous piece of jewelry inside. He took her on lavish trips, and she was able to buy all the Ferragamo shoes she wanted.

He was a big smoker, like so many businessmen were in the early eighties, and was rarely without a cigarette in hand. Even though my father quit smoking in his late fifties, the smell of cigarette smoke still sparks loving memories of him. My parents were madly in love back then and still are to this very day after fifty-eight years of marriage.

# Chapter 1

I still catch my father giving my mom a gentle pat on the tush when he walks by her, and they just simply take care of each other, in various ways that seem effortless.

My father wasn't around the house very much when I was a child; he would leave for work very early each morning and return home late. However, he made it a priority to give each of us his undivided attention when he was home. He always tried to make it to every sporting event my twin brothers were involved in, my sister's horse shows, or my dance recitals. Some of my favorite childhood memories are of when my father and I would drive into the big city on the weekend to see the giant skyscraper where his office was located. I would play secretary outside his office while he did whatever work needed to be done, gazing out the window in amazement at the vast Houston skyline.

Our home was in an upper-class neighborhood on the outskirts of Houston, Texas. It looked like a mini White House with four tall white pillars in the front, a perfectly manicured lawn and numerous towering pine trees surrounding the perimeter. The house was a large two-story home. My sister, two brothers and I all had our own bedrooms upstairs, while my parents' bedroom was tucked away downstairs. There was a guest room and even a game room with a pool table and big circular bar that hosted plenty of parties over the years. The backyard had a sparkling blue swimming pool surrounded by a large deck where my mother would often be sunbathing her already perfectly tanned skin. It was always the most festive house on the block at Christmas and the scariest on Halloween. Everyone in the neighborhood knew each other, kids rode their bikes everywhere and spent summers playing barefoot outside all day until the streetlights came on. There is not one thing I would change about my childhood.

One day in 1984, my father came home, announced he was retiring from the oil business and that we were moving back to Farmington, New Mexico, the small town where I was born.

"Why Farmington, of all places?" I asked my parents, a little stunned as we sat at the kitchen table.

My mother cheerfully chimed in, "We have had enough of the big city and are ready to slow things down a bit now that Dad has decided to retire, sweetie. I know you will love it! It's not far from Colorado, and you can ski anytime you want."

Well, that was good enough for me, and just like that, I was on board with this huge, life-changing event. I was fourteen years old, and my brothers and sister had already gone off to college, so I was basically an only child at this point. My parents were ready for a change from the hussle and bussle of the big city and traffic, and ready for the slower pace of small town life they had known and loved.

It's funny to think back at just how traumatic and scary that should have been for me, but I was actually excited for this new chapter. I didn't feel an ounce of fear, maybe because up until that point fear was something I had never truly experienced. The worst fear I had dealt with was watching the movie *Helter Skelter* as a kid. I knew I would miss my friends in Houston, but wasn't concerned about making new ones and was eager for the challenge.

I quickly discovered just how different Farmington was from Houston, as I looked out the window of the tiny plane. I saw nothing but brown. Everything was brown. The grass, the leafless trees, the dirt, the flat-top mesas. It all just looked so brown, dreary and dead. It was December and bitter cold, so very different from warm and humid Texas weather. As the plane touched down at the small, one-level airport, a strange wave of fear washed over me. I felt like I was an alien that had just landed on another planet. I was not prepared for how different things would look and how different I would feel.

*This is going to be very interesting*, I thought with a small sense of panic.

# Chapter 1

The minute I stepped foot into my new school a few days later, dread entered my entire body. It was nothing like the beautiful brand-new middle school I had attended in Houston. This school was an old, one-story building that looked as if it would crumble to the ground at any second. The classrooms smelled like a cross between mothballs and old socks, the desks had rusty metal legs, and the library was always freezing cold. Like most schools, they assigned someone to be your "buddy," which is sort of sad for all involved when you think about it, having someone forced to be your friend when you're the new kid.

I remember everyone staring at me with a strange curiosity. They were so fascinated that the new girl was from Texas, they all wanted to hear my accent. I assumed it was because new kids were a rarity, and I quietly wondered, why would anyone live in, much less move to, such a depressing place? My heart ached for the comfort and security of my old life in Texas. I missed the green trees, warm air, and the familiar, friendly faces of my friends in the hallways at school. I suddenly missed them more than anything else in the world.

After a few months of crying every day after school and begging my parents to PLEASE move back to Texas, things slowly became more bearable. I tried out for the cheer team the following year and made it. I became friends with the girls on the squad, and things were starting to look up. Farmington was slowly starting to feel like home. But things changed dramatically my sophomore year, or maybe more accurately, I changed dramatically. That summer I grew three inches, got my braces off, and learned how to transform my hair to the perfect shade of blonde.

My body still had some developing to do, but I could sense curiosity in the boys' staring eyes. I had no idea how to handle all this new and foreign attention from the most popular boys in school. In my mind, I was still the awkward, goofy, skinny girl who boys paid zero attention to. While I used to be invisible to them, now I was the girl they looked at and pursued. This was all new to me; boys had never really flirted with me or actually tried to get my attention before, and I really didn't know how to respond to it. I couldn't tell if I liked it or hated it.

Before long, it became very clear the older girls in school were not very happy that I was stealing the attention of "their" boys, and they let me know it in a big way. My car was keyed, and horrible words like "slut" and "Sarah gives head" were written in shoe polish for all the school to see. I didn't even know what "head" meant at the time, and rumors about me spread like wildfire. If I went to a party on the weekend and was alone with a boy at the party, the assumption was that we had sex or did other things that I had never heard of. These boys were older star athletes, everyone worshipped them and believed anything they said. It got so bad that I lost most of my friends. I just assumed they didn't want everyone to think they were associated with the school slut. I was so lonely that I eventually gave in to their advances, trying to find the acceptance I was craving. At the time, I thought the older boys were my friends, but in reality I was more like a project to them. In a way, I came to live up to my reputation because it was the only thing that felt good at the time and distracted me from the hatred the older girls handed me.

I was fifteen years old when I had sex for the first time, and I hated myself for it. I hadn't even started my period yet, I was physically still a child and was in no way ready for the emotional or physical repercussions. I was doing very adult things, with the mind and body that was not quite ready yet. I was on an emotional roller coaster, scared to go to school, while at the same time craving the positive attention from anyone who would give it to me, it was a vicious cycle. The more the older boys talked to me; the meaner the girls got. I was always on high alert for the next comment aimed at me, yelled across the quad for all to hear, or who was waiting around the corner in the halls for the chance to insult me to my face.

# Chapter 1

The bullying got even worse in 1986 at the end of my sophomore year and continued into 1987. I was actually afraid to go to school and did everything I could just to blend in. I wanted so badly to be invisible again, but at almost six feet tall, that was a virtually impossible task. I was on the dance team at that time, and the mean girls would throw all kinds of stadium food at me. I distinctly remember getting hit in the face by a hot dog as we marched onto the field to perform at halftime, but I hardly flinched when I felt the smack. Even though pure humiliation seared through me and tears poured down my face, I continued to march like nothing had happened, keenly aware of the laughter from my tormentors in the stands. My parents were always at the games to watch me dance, but where they sat was so far from the student section, they never noticed a thing. I did make a few friends on the dance team and was grateful they seemed to not be bothered by how hated I was by the older students. I became really good at not talking about what was happening to me and prayed every day no one would see the next violation.

I was too ashamed to ask for help or talk to my parents about the demoralizing things that were being done to me. I felt dirty and embarrassed at who I had become, and by this time my self-worth was nonexistent. I know now I could have easily gone to my parents for help, and I am sure they would have done anything for me; but as a teenage girl, I was more afraid of them finding out what I was doing sexually. I even wondered if in some way, I deserved what was happening to me.

It was one of the most difficult times in my life even to this day, and I am no stranger to hard times. Just writing about the events that happened more than thirty years ago, still brings to life the same sense of fear and self-hatred. The word *bully* wasn't really used back then, and there were no "anti-bullying campaigns" like there are now in school. I can attest to the destruction it can cause, as well as the painful emotional scars that last a lifetime.

Twice that year I was sexually assaulted. No, I was not pinned down and raped, kicking and screaming like I thought assault was back then, and both very different from each other. The first time, one of the popular boys drove me out to a place called "the hills" during lunch. We had what was called *open lunch* and could leave campus for an hour. I was excited and naively thought we were actually just going to lunch together. I remember nervously asking him where we were going to eat. He just looked at me with a cat-about-to-eat-the-canary look and said not to worry about it, that it was a surprise. Once we got there, he put the car in Park and turned to look at me. We were out in the middle of nowhere, and I suddenly became very nervous by the look on his face. He quickly climbed on top of me in the passenger seat of his tiny two-seater, unzipped his pants and proceeded to ejaculate all over my shirt. I was stunned—the whole event felt like it lasted less than a few seconds. Just as quickly as it started, he climbed off of me, and not a single word was said by either of us all the way back to school. Once we got back to school, I went straight to the restroom to wash my shirt and sat in the stall, missing class as it dried, feeling nothing but pure humiliation. Once again, I felt I must have deserved it because I chose to go to lunch with him.

The second assault was different than the first, but actually worse in my eyes, and it affected me for a long time. I had gone to a boy's house for a get-together that he was hosting. It seemed fine to me because I knew most of the people he said he was having over. I came straight from a babysitting job, only to find that he was the only one in the house. When I arrived, he asked me to go to the back of the house because he had something for me. I reluctantly followed him, thinking he must have a cool new stereo or something like that to show me.

We got to his parents bedroom when he said, "This is what I want to show you." He turned around, grabbed my hand and put it on the crotch of his pants. He pushed me onto the bed and started kissing me aggressively while holding my hand in place. That was when I heard laughter coming from his parents' closet. I managed to jump from the bed and open the closet door to find four or five boys hiding inside with a large video camera in hand.

"Oh my God, what is going on?" My voice was trembling so much I could hardly understand my own words. Clearly there was not a party going on, they were planning on videotaping what they assumed was going to happen. I ran as fast as I could from that house. I can only imagine how my life would have been affected had their mission been accomplished.

It is a violation that is hard for me to explain, even now. Some might even disagree that it rises to the level of sexual assault, but whatever it was, it stayed with me my entire life. My heart aches for all the women who have endured far worse than I did, most likely keeping it to themselves and feeling like it was their fault as well. I feel certain those two minor events changed my entire path in my relationships with men.

That year changed me in a million different ways, and I plunged into such a dark place that I feared I would never climb out. I lost my innocence, I lost my friends, I lost my confidence and my free spirit. But most all, I lost my ability to trust. I never told a soul when it happened. I held it all inside; it was only years later that I told my family.

That year was the first time I casually thought about suicide. I now understand there is no such thing as casually thinking about suicide. I thought about pulling into my garage with the tiny remains of those degrading words still painted on my car, closing the garage door and letting the engine run. It would be painless and quick. I fantasized about what my bullies would do when they woke up to the news I had killed myself. Would they laugh and be happy, or would they feel a tinge of remorse? I wondered what all the boys who hurt me would think; would they feel any guilt? But I also thought about my family and how broken they would be if I actually did it. The love I had for my family was the only thing keeping me alive, and so

I kept willing myself to get up and endure yet another humiliating day at school.

It was only after I had become a senior that I felt free from my tormentors. By then, they had all graduated and things became a little better for my last year in high school; however, the emotional damage remained deep inside. I became co-captain of the dance team, joined the drama club and had real friendships with a few girls. I thrived when I was on stage and did it as much as possible. I loved being someone other than myself. I fell in love with acting, and I knew it was something I wanted to pursue in my adult life. I loved the freedom of diving into different characters, and my fellow drama club members accepted me just the way I was. I even had a real boyfriend who wanted me for more than just sex. I finally felt like a normal teenager.

Despite things improving at school through activities, friends, and having a serious boyfriend, I could not get out of that town fast enough. Looking back on my high school years, I have very mixed emotions. For a long time I thought Farmington was a horrible place; but in reality it was more about the people doing horrible things to me, not so much the place. Farmington is actually quite beautiful for a small town. It has a laid-back, easy vibe. I now understand why people love it and see why my parents wanted to retire there. Many of my high school friends live in Farmington to this day and have raised their own families there. It wasn't Farmington that hurt me, it was a handful of people that did. So in 1988, I decided to make my escape.

CHAPTER 2

Two weeks after graduating from high school, I packed up the red Ford Probe sports car my dad surprised me with for graduation. I hugged my parents tightly as tears welled up in my eyes. My dad went over the map he had so lovingly highlighted for me one more time, and my mom made me promise to call from a pay phone at each of my stops during the eight-hour drive. I would be starting summer classes at Arizona State University in Tempe, Arizona, with only a few days to settle into my newly furnished dorm room before classes started. I was beyond thrilled to live in a place where nobody knew anything about me, and for the first time in years, I could just be myself in this new warm and sunny place.

I instantly fell in love with Arizona. I loved how the sun shined every day, and the 100-degree or more weather didn't bother me in the slightest. Even the fast food restaurants had gorgeous flower pots in front, and streets and sidewalks were spotless. Everyone was beautiful there, and people seemed to always be in a good mood. Probably from the massive amounts of vitamin D in the form of sunshine we were all soaking up.

I used my six-foot frame to my advantage and signed on with The Elite Agency, one of the top modeling agencies in the country. I had just won second runner-up in the "Elite Look of the Year" contest and was working on entering the Miss Arizona USA Pageant, which had been a huge dream of mine since I was a little girl. I had just pledged a sorority and was starting to make strong, meaningful friendships with those girls as well. My confidence was slowly but surely coming back, and I was the happiest I had been in a very long time. I hardly gave Farmington a second thought.

Even though I loved the college experience, it was academically challenging for me. I wasn't really the studious type and struggled in my classes. Sadly for my parents who were paying my tuition, I just stopped going to class. I thought that college wouldn't really matter, considering the career path I wanted to take. I am sure my parents were disappointed that I wasn't doing well in my classes; but as usual, they supported whatever I wanted to do with my life, with words of encouragement to follow my dreams.

I had my life all planned out and knew two things for certain: I wanted to be a star, and I wanted to be a wife and mother. I had found my passion being on stage or a runway and loved all the glamour it provided. I was also keenly aware of how much I wanted my own family, even at a young age. My game plan was to become a mega superstar first, then I would meet and marry my hunky, superstar husband and we would have three or four super cute star babies. I had it all figured out and had absolutely no doubt that was exactly how my life would be.

One weekend in early 1989, my high school boyfriend Sean came to Arizona for a visit from Farmington. Sean and I were very serious during my senior year in high school, and I was as much in love with him as any eighteen-year-old could be. He was a couple of years older than me and was pretty well known around town as the good-looking star football player from the neighboring small town of Bloomingdale.

## Chapter 2

He was tall and well built with beautiful hazel eyes, dark hair and a quiet personality. But he was also the bad boy who liked to get into fights, drink, and smoke cigarettes and pot on a regular basis. This was a bit scandalous being that he was from a very Mormon family. But, by the time we started dating, he had slowed down a little and was trying to get his life together after graduating high school. I knew I would miss him when I left Farmington but I also knew I needed to pursue a different life path, and it didn't look like he was going to accompany me on that path.

We broke up on good terms right before I left for Arizona and vowed to try and see each other when we could, no strings attached. As much as I loved him, I knew I could not stay in Farmington, and he had no plans of ever leaving. But the moment I opened my dorm room door, my heart instantly fell into the all-familiar feeling of love that was so strong in high school. He looked extra gorgeous that day standing in the front doorway of my small kitchen. He made ripped-up jeans look cool before ripped-up jeans were even a thing and could rock a backward baseball hat. He wore a sleeveless t-shirt that showed off his well-tanned, muscular arms, courtesy of the construction job he had over the summer. We certainly didn't act broken up during that visit, and he went back to Farmington very happy and probably a little tired.

Let's just say the couple of times I'd forgotten to take my pill caught up with me. I was already three months along before it was confirmed. I never even noticed I'd missed a period, I just wrote it off to stress or too many college parties. I went home to Farmington for Christmas that year and never returned to school in Arizona. My mom was actually thrilled at the news that she would soon become a grandmother, while I could tell my father was worried about Sean and if he was going to make anything of himself. I am sure they both had better plans about who my future husband would be, but they were supportive and optimistic that all would work out. My father did have a little chat with Sean one night shortly before the wedding.

"Son, I need you to promise me that you will go to college," my father said kindly.

"Yes, sir, I promise. And I promise to take good care of Sarah forever." It was actually a very real and heartfelt moment with my parents in our living room, and I believed we were doing the right thing, especially now that Sean had agreed to go back to school.

Sean and I were married in my parents' home in Farmington just after the holidays in 1989. My long blonde hair hung beautifully French-braided down my back, and I wore a cream-colored, tea-length dress trimmed with lace, mindful of being conservative for our Mormon guests. I have to laugh about that now, being that I was already knocked up, which clearly meant we had sex before marriage. There was no denying why we were getting married so young, as my baby bump was more of a baby mound by this time and difficult to disguise. But I was happy, I was in love and I was certain that everything was going to be just fine. Sean's father, who was a bishop in the Mormon Church, married us in front of a few family and friends as we stood in the archway of my parents' dining room. My mother had taken such care to make everything so beautiful that I didn't even feel like I was in my own home as Sean slid the simple gold band on my finger and we said, "I do."

After the shock of having a baby at nineteen years old wore off, I was eager to start my new chapter and couldn't wait to meet the little life growing inside me. While my dreams of becoming an actress or supermodel had to be put to rest, I was at least going to be the mom I knew I wanted to be, even if it was a tad early.

Just as Sean had promised my father, he enrolled in college at Brigham Young University in Provo, Utah. I had never been to Utah and was up for the adventure as we packed up our cars and a small U-Haul with the few pieces of furniture given to us. I remember having a flashback as we pulled out of the driveway of my parents' home. Less than a year ago, I had pulled out of that same driveway in my brand-new red sports car; now I was in a more family-friendly, used, four-door Pontiac. My life had dramatically changed in such a short period of time, this time I was a little scared to be leaving my parents. I suddenly felt like a little girl who just wanted her mommy, and now I was about to become one.

We lasted about two months in Provo. I hated it there, was terribly homesick, and school was not working out for Sean. I was terrified of having a baby away from my family in a place that felt like a foreign country and wanted to go home so badly. My dad reached out to a friend, asking if he would hire Sean to work for his pipeline company, with the promise he would take classes at the local community college. We packed up once again and headed back to Farmington. This time I wasn't even too upset about having to move back there, even though it still felt like hell on earth to me. At least we had both of our families close by to help us navigate the journey into parenthood.

Hayley Jane was born August 22, 1989, and was absolutely perfect in every way. She came so quickly there wasn't even time for an epidural, not quite part of my game plan, but worth every painful second. As I held her in my arms for the first time, I could not believe how beautiful she was with her cherub face and beautiful brown eyes. I was overwhelmed with joy, gratitude and maybe a little fear that I was now responsible for this tiny human. I was a mommy for the first time and knew things would never be as they once were.

I don't think any new mom is really ready for what it is like to have a baby. As young as I was, I thought babies just wanted to snuggle and coo all the time, take naps when you wanted them to nap and sleep through the night after the first month or so. I know for a fact that I could not have survived without the help of my parents. Looking back, I know I struggled with postpartum depression for a short time.

I would sit for hours in the rocking chair of our tiny, dark apartment with tears flowing nonstop.

Eventually, I started a part-time job at a small insurance company owned by the parents of a dear friend from high school. Kyle was my first crush at fourteen when we moved to Farmington, but we mostly stayed best friends over the years. I was very close with Kyle's mother, who adored Hayley as if she was her very own granddaughter. Thankfully, she offered me a job answering phones at the small insurance company for a little extra money. I couldn't wait to leave for work the minute my mother came over to stay with Hayley and loved being around other adults at the office for a few hours every day.

As all my friends were coming home for college breaks, going to parties and out dancing, I was home with a baby who seemed to never sleep. I remember feeling heavy with sadness at times, even though I loved Hayley with every ounce of my being. I was ashamed of these confusing feelings and never discussed it with anyone; was it normal to feel this way? I thought maybe it was my age and the fact that my marriage was starting to turn in the wrong direction.

I am so grateful that my dark time with depression did not last long, and I soon started feeling like my old self again. Hayley was my whole world as my marriage quickly unraveled. Sean was a good man, but he had a drug issue that, unfortunately, continued to get worse. Pot became something he did first thing in the morning on most days and the last thing he did at night. His idea of a fun Saturday night would be sitting in a friend's basement drinking beer and smoking. He was content being a laborer barely making more than minimum wage.

One week we were so short on money that we didn't have enough cash to buy diapers. I had one diaper left to get Hayley through the night to the next morning. I laid her on the floor with a towel around her tiny body. That towel got us through until bedtime when I could finally put that last diaper on. My mom often brought diapers over when she came to babysit, but I was always too proud to ask for help. Thankfully, she came the next morning with a pack of diapers in hand; she must have read my mind. I never would have dreamed the year before, just how exciting seeing a package of diapers would be!

I was not at all interested in converting to the Mormon church. Unfortunately, this caused a wedge to form on his side of the family, and was an always-present point of pressure. When I would attend church with Sean and his family, I always felt like an outsider. It seemed to me that women were expected to sort of just sit, be quiet and support their men, who seemed to be held in a higher regard. I felt myself resenting this more and more each day, and I knew I no longer loved Sean the way I should. After less than two years of marriage, just after my twenty-first birthday, I decided I had to leave him. I wanted so much more for Hayley and me, and I could not help but worry about our future. I started to feel the walls of Farmington, New Mexico, closing in all around me once again. I needed to get out as soon as possible.

The divorce was quick and final a few months later without much of a fight. We had a whopping two hundred dollars in our checking account and no other assets to our names beside our own cars. Hayley and I packed up and moved back to Houston, Texas. We settled into a three-bedroom apartment with my brother Steve, who was kind enough to take us in. I loved being near my older twin brothers, they are the funniest two guys ever, and we have always had a close bond. They were twenty-eight years old, 6'3", handsome, and living life to the fullest. Steve was a bachelor, and I am sure he was happy to have me around to tidy up and cook from time to time. He was kind enough to stay with Hayley if I wanted to go out. I'm sure people in our apartment complex thought we were a happy young couple with a cute little girl.

My other brother Jeff and his girlfriend Melissa, who is now my sister-in law and adore with all my heart, also helped with Hayley whenever I needed it. I loved that our new apartment, which was a classic brick, two story complex that was right across the street from The Galleria, one of the largest malls in the U.S., complete with an ice-skating rink right in the middle.

I tried to ignore the guilt I felt for moving so far away from Hayley's father; I knew he loved us the best he could. The desire for a better life was much too strong to fight, and I felt right at home back in the big city where I'd grown up, far away from Farmington. I knew visits would be hard for Sean, as money was scarce for us both, but I just figured we would work it all out as we went along.

With the help of my parents and my leftover college money, I entered beauty school and began to pursue my new life and career as a single mother.

CHAPTER 3

I WORKED HARD DURING that year in beauty school. I dated a ton and was juggling the single parent thing pretty well. My parents visited us often. They were, and still are, a big influence in Hayley's life. Even with all the fun I was having, I started to ache for a real, long-term relationship. I never had trouble meeting anyone, but as soon as they found out I was twenty-one with a two-year-old, well, that usually took care of anything serious moving forward.

After I graduated from beauty school, I quickly landed my first job as an assistant to a French hairstylist in a trendy, upscale salon just around the corner from our apartment. By then I was twenty-two, and Hayley was an adorable three-year-old who stole everyone's heart with her big brown eyes and sweet disposition. I had started dating a guy named Ben. He was the first guy who didn't run for the hills when he learned that I had a daughter. He was good friends with both my brothers, very handsome, and I felt safe with him. We always had a great time when we went out, but really weren't thinking much beyond that.

In December of 1992, Ben casually asked me if I would set his friend up with my girlfriend, Megan, for a double date. His friend's

name was Greg Swindell, and apparently he was some famous baseball player who had just signed a lucrative contract with the Houston
Astros. I was told Greg had been all over the local news and that he
was the newest addition, along with Doug Drabek, to the Astros' big
*one-two punch* the team was looking for.

I called Megan and teasingly told her, "You owe me for this one!
Better go shopping for a new outfit in case you get on the news!" She
was all in and I was excited for her.

We all planned to meet at my apartment for drinks before going
out. Expecting that the first knock at the door would be Megan, I was
surprised to see Greg in the doorway as the first to arrive. I am a noto-
riously early bird myself, so I was dressed and ready with a smile and
a glass of wine in hand.

"Hi, you must be Greg, come on in!" My voice sounded a little
more excited than it should have.

"Hi, nice to meet you, Sarah." I immediately thought, oh no,
I am in **BIG** trouble. My stomach literally flipped, and I felt my face
turn hot the second we shook hands. There was an immediate energy
between us, and I almost couldn't find the words to tell him to come
in. He was tall, with a strong, husky build which was right up my ally.
He was soft spoken and had an air of confidence, but not cockiness.
All I remember is how great he looked in his tight, pressed jeans, crisp
button-down shirt and cowboy boots, with lips so perfect that I was
already thinking about what it would be like to kiss them. We also
had one major thing in common. He also had a little girl from his first
marriage, and suddenly I was no longer the only person in my circle
of friends with a child.

Happy everyone else was late, we soon all piled into Greg's brand-
new red pickup truck and headed to dinner. We sat at a cozy table for
four, and soon Greg and I quickly fell into natural conversation, laughing;
about what, I can't begin to remember. I almost forgot we were with

other people at the table until Ben said something to grab our attention and brought us back to the reality that we were not alone on the date.

After dinner, we headed to our favorite country bar for more drinks and dancing. I was glad my friend Megan, who was originally from New York, didn't know how to two-step, and Ben was not a fan either. When Greg asked me if I could two-step, I was thrilled to show off my well-developed skills. I know it sounds a bit cliché, but I felt like we were the only two people on the dance floor. It was something I had never felt before, and I wanted that moment to go on forever. I loved the way he smelled, how his eyes melted into mine as we danced, and how he held me so close it almost made me weak in the knees. After what seemed like forever, we came back to earth and realized we should get off the dance floor noticing the looks on our dates' faces.

We headed back to my apartment where everyone had parked their cars, chatted for a while in the parking lot, then everyone started to say their goodbyes. I watched Megan and Greg walk to his truck together. She giggled with obvious flirtation and climbed into the passenger seat. They were going back to his place together, and I did not like it one bit.

The next morning, I was jolted awake by the sound of the phone ringing. I answered with hesitation, already guessing it was Megan wanting to give me the whole play-by-play of her evening with Greg. She was bursting with a giddy energy. "Oh my gosh!" she squealed with delight, "he is Aaaammmmazing!"

She told me all about her night with him, what a good kisser he was, how cool his high-rise condo was, and how much she liked him. I nervously asked, "Did you sleep with him?"

I held my breath for the response. "No, but hot damn we played around a lot!" I suddenly felt a rush of relief run through me. After we hung up, I called my mom and told her tearfully, " I think I just set up the love of my life with my friend." I could not get Greg out of my mind, and it was sort of freaking me out.

A few days later, the four of us went out again. It is funny that I don't remember much about what happened on the second date, but what happened after the date is clear as a bell. Ben and Megan both had to be somewhere early the next day, so the three of them walked to the parking lot of my apartment together at the end of the night. As soon as they got in their cars, Greg turned to look up at me still standing on my balcony. With a huge smile, he motioned with his hand that said, "I'm coming back."

Sure enough, a few minutes later Greg pulled back into my complex and knocked on my door. My hand was shaking as I opened it and saw him standing there with a sweet smile as I took his hand and lead him inside. Then, without saying a word, we had our first kiss. The kiss I had been longing for and thought might never come.

"I have been thinking about this all night, I am so into you it's crazy." Yep, as you can probably guess, I melted right then and there. We somehow ended up on my floor, all tangled up and making out like crazy teenagers for what seemed like hours. Our clothes managed to stay on, as we both seemed content with the passion only our kissing was creating. We hardly spoke a word, we didn't need to as our hands explored each other's bodies, generating a delicious urgency; we were careful not to go too far. It was almost as if we wanted to drag the feeling out as long as we possibly could, never wanting it to end.

"This is so wrong to do to our friends, they have no idea!" I said when things cooled down a little and we came back to earth.

"There is no way they DON'T have an idea," he said with a sheepish grin.

Needless to say, Ben and Megan could sense something was happening, and eventually the questions started coming. As much as we tried to deny anything was going on between us, it was impossible to ignore. Greg playfully told Ben he'd better not go out of town anytime soon or he was going to steal me away.

## Chapter 3

Well, Ben did end up going out of town, and I was definitely stolen. After the night of our first kiss, we never went another day without seeing each other. Greg would come by the salon when I was working and had more shampoos done in one week than anyone I knew. Any excuse he could find to see me, he found it. Our chemistry was off the charts; just being near him made my whole body react in ways it never had before. At work I felt like I was literally floating around the salon because my heart was filled with so much love, and even my coworkers could see it.

Our love was growing fast and furious, showing no signs of slowing down. I wondered, how did a guy like him, love someone like me? I was also aware of the whispers behind my back. I once heard one of Greg's friends refer to me as a "cleat chaser," and I'm sure people probably assumed I was a gold digger, being that I was a hairdresser with a child. In my eyes, Greg was so much more than just a professional baseball player with a lot of money. He was the most romantic, caring, funny and sexiest man I had ever been around in my entire life. He pursued me much more than I pursued him because I was careful to guard my heart. He treated me with a kindness that made me feel like I was the most special person in the world to him, and I was crazy in love. Best of all, he adored Hayley, and she was just as crazy for him.

My heart would race and my palms would sweat just seeing him pull up to the salon or when he would pick me up for a date. The fact that he happened to have money was just a bonus. It's sort of like flying coach to Italy with the love of your life, then finding out you both got upgraded to first class. I was still going to Italy, it was just going to be a much more comfortable flight!

I knew Greg would be leaving for spring training soon, as the off-season was coming to an end. He would be going to Florida for six weeks, and I had to wonder what would happen to us being apart for so long. Would he break up with me, or would we stay in touch while he was gone? I was scared to bring the question up because I was not sure what the answer would be. It was a big year for him, and I did not want to be a distraction or something that would bring him down. But he made it clear that he wanted nothing more than to have me in his life.

CHAPTER 4

SEVEN WEEKS AFTER OUR first date, I stood looking into the mirror of the marble-covered bathroom in our suite at the Beach Club Resort on the Disney World property in Orlando, Florida. Hot rollers were piled high on my head, and my new Ann Taylor cream-colored dress was hanging on the door behind me, tags still attached. New matching pumps sat neatly in their box and on the counter next to the pearl earrings my sister-in-law, Melissa, wore at her wedding the year before.

Talk about a whirlwind, I could not believe how much and how quickly my life had changed in just seven weeks. It was 1993, I was twenty-three years old and about to get married for the second time during the Houston Astros' spring training.

As I stood there in the bathroom, I thought back to the engagement and how it still felt like a dream. It was a typical Wednesday and not unusual for Greg to come into the salon while I was working. But instead of talking to me as I worked, he pulled me aside by the soda machine. He took my hands into his, and he was sweating nervously as he looked straight into my eyes. He proceeded to pull out a tiny black velvet box and slowly opened it. Inside was the most beautiful diamond ring I had ever seen. He looked at me without saying a single word, but with tears in his eyes. I looked up at him as my heart lept and said, "Is this, is this . . . ?" and without letting me finish my thought, he nodded his head with a vigorous *yes*.

A few days later, Greg called my boss at the salon to ask permission to take me to spring training for six weeks and if I could have that time off. Greg flew my parents in to watch Hayley for a few weeks before the three of them would join us in Florida. I didn't even own a decent suitcase or clothes, for that matter, so my mom and I had a last-minute shopping spree before I left town as Greg Swindell's new fiancée.

Being with Greg sometimes felt like I was living a Hollywood movie. He was a celebrity around town, and we received star treatment everywhere we went. People would stop him in the mall for an autograph or picture, or come up to our table at a restaurant just to shake his hand and wish him luck for the upcoming baseball season. Even with all of the attention he was getting, he always made it a priority to make me feel like I was the only thing that mattered. The only person he wanted to give any of his attention to was me, and I loved every sweet second of it.

Looking back, I should have felt at least a little hesitation about how fast we were moving, but I didn't. Greg's divorce from his first wife, Molly, had not even been finalized yet, they were in the middle of messy paperwork and custody details for their two-year-old daughter, Shelby. Our girls got along beautifully, Shelby was two and Hayley was three. Other than his ex-wife understandably not being too thrilled about how fast things were moving, I had absolutely no hesitation about any of it.

At twenty-three, I never thought about how painful it all must have been for Molly. While I was not the cause of their divorce, as they had already filed by the time we met, I certainly did not help make her situation any less painful. I wish I would have been more sensitive to her situation and more understanding about why she was making it so difficult for us, or so it seemed to me, when we wanted to have their daughter stay with us. Now that I am older and have been through the very same situation, I know how crushing it is to see the man you love choose another woman over you.

After living through gut-wrenching custody situations with Hayley and her father, I knew what was happening with Greg's own daughter, and Molly would be extremely difficult to deal with. There was a lot of arguing and tears between the two of them. He felt that his daughter was caught in the middle, just like Hayley had been. The back and forth went on for a long time, and the stress was taking a toll on everyone. At one point, it was suggested that it might be better for everyone if we just let go and allow Shelby and Molly to move forward without us in their lives. Molly had just remarried to a wonderful man, and everyone just wanted peace.

My life has plenty of regrets and wishful do-overs, and this situation is at the top of that list. At the time, we thought we were doing what was best for everyone. Looking back, we should never have agreed to let Greg's daughter go. Maybe we did do the right thing, but we will never truly know for sure. All I know is that I have no doubt Greg's daughter must have felt as if we didn't want her; most importantly, that her dad didn't want her. I can't imagine how she must have felt when she was old enough to know that Greg had moved along to live a life with a new family. It's terrible to even write about this now, and I almost didn't. After a conversation with Greg during the process of writing this book, we felt that we had to be completely honest about *everything*, including the shameful stuff, and Greg wanted me to share this part of our story.

At that time so many years ago, we both believed we did the right thing by not having her go back and forth from house to house with parents who could hardly even speak to each other. We saw the relief in Hayley's life once that stopped for her, but it didn't come without a price to pay down the road for both girls and for the entire family. Hayley and Shelby spent a year together as tiny children. We have an entire photo album filled with just the two of them playing together and enjoying life as sisters.

I think if the adults would have worked harder, things would have become better over time, but sadly we will never know. Not only did we lose Greg's daughter, an entire family never got to know their half-sister, granddaughter, aunt, and so on. I know Greg has been wracked with guilt from that decision over the years, and he thinks about her all the time. I know if we both could have that do-over, being in his daughter's life would be number one on that list. I know Greg's wish, as well as mine, is that someday we will all have a relationship and that she will meet the family that has never stopped thinking about her. We have heard that she is happy and has had a beautiful life, which makes it a little less difficult to accept the decision we made so many years ago.

On my wedding day in 1993, I never dreamed that life could get any better than it was at that very moment, even with all the moving parts that were swirling around me.

Our tiny wedding was an intimate ceremony at a resort on the Disneyland property in a simple white gazebo. It was a beautiful warm and sunny spring day, and all the flowers on the grounds were bursting with vibrant color. With only a few family members in attendance, Hayley stood right beside us, looking as cute as ever in the floral print dress with a big bow in the back that she helped pick out the day before. We stood hand in hand as we recited our vows while tears welled up in our eyes. I was filled with so much love, it was almost too overwhelming to hold all the emotion in.

Right after he slid the ring onto my finger, Greg suddenly said, "Wait, there is one more thing I need to do." Greg reached into his inside pocket and pulled out a tiny gold ring with a pink stone in the middle. He took Hayley's little hand and put the ring on her finger, just as he had done with me moments earlier.

"Now I am complete," Greg said with a smile.

It was one of the most magical days of my life, and I will truly never forget it. Sadly, my brother had forgotten our camcorder in the house we had rented for spring training and only had one of those throw-away cameras for still pictures. To this day, that one grainy photo is more than enough. It still sits comfortably in the same frame I placed it in the moment I had it developed and is the only decent photo we have of our wedding.

That night we invited all the players and staff of the Houston Astros, along with a few players from the Cleveland Indians, to a private party at a club on Disney property that Greg had rented for the night. The promise of new love, a new baseball season, and the beginning of a spectacular time in my own life filled the air. At the end of the evening, Greg and I spent our first night together as husband and wife. Exhausted, a little drunk and more in love than I ever thought possible, we fell asleep in each other's arms.

Shortly after the wedding, spring training came to an end, and it was time to fly back to Houston, Texas, as a new family. The entire city was buzzing with excitement to see what was ahead for their beloved Astros and the new players who had joined the team. While we were in Florida, Greg had decided that we needed a proper home when we got back, and our realtor had sent us several flyers of homes for sale in the West University area of town. Back then, there was no such thing as *Realtor.com*, or even the internet for that matter, so we happily house-hunted the old-fashioned way.

After only one day of looking, we found the perfect home on a quaint, tree-lined street in the West University neighborhood, just a few miles from the Astrodome. West U, as it is casually known around town, is different than other areas of Houston. The lots are small, but all the homes have a Southern charm to them with each one being different than the next. Nothing like the huge master-planned communities that seem to be taking over the entire state of Texas now. You might see a tiny old one-story with a classic front porch right next door to a giant remodeled two-story with plantation shutters and a wraparound balcony.

Ours was a gray two-story stucco home with white shutters and the generous front porch I had always wanted. It wasn't a giant home, but large enough so we could immediately start adding to our family, which we were very actively working on. I remember thinking over and over again how incredibly lucky I was to be so in love and finally moving out of my old, dark apartment into a gorgeous new home with my new husband. The moving process quickly began, and I loved every minute of it. This may have been the start of my moving addiction. I loved everything about the transformation of turning an empty house into a beautiful home and the sense of accomplishment when it was all done.

I loved unpacking (I know there must be something seriously wrong with me) and getting everything organized and put away in its proper place. I became so good at moving over the years that it was common knowledge that by the end of move-in day, I would have everything unpacked, pictures hung, music playing and candles burning. My favorite part was always having my mom right beside me, helping to organize with skill that would make Martha Stewart proud. My favorite memories of my mom are of us working together in whatever new home we were moving in to, while listening to The Backstreet Boys, or the latest boy band that was popular at the time, as we unpacked. We drank wine as we worked and chatted about life and didn't stop until everything was complete. I think I lost count around twenty-seven moves; it must be over thirty at this point. Trust me, I am scratching my head even typing this. Clearly there is some hidden reason for my love of moving that only a licensed therapist can uncover.

But, let's go back to 1993 to the first of many homes the Swindell family would have. My parents were living in Albuquerque, New Mexico, at that time and agreed to come to Houston and stay at Greg's condo for a while to help us with Hayley. They were thrilled to be a part of this exciting time, adored Greg, and they felt pretty cool staying in their new celebrity son-in-law's high-rise. In a matter of just a few months, I went from barely making ends meet, making a hundred dollars a week, to money not being an issue at all. Greg gave me his credit card to get all new clothes, shoes, purses, and anything I wanted to furnish our new home.

"Don't worry about a thing, babe! I trust your taste in making our house perfect," Greg playfully said when I asked him about a budget for furnishing our new home. "Just put anything you want on the card," as he handed me his American Express.

I had never had a credit card before, other than using my mom's Dillards card on occasion when I needed clothes for Hayley when I was single. My mom and I had a blast furniture shopping at the Houston Design Center and cute little furniture boutiques in West U. The Amex card and I quickly became dear friends.

Greg and I both received new cars from a dealership in Houston, in return for doing a commercial, and were on the cover of *West U Magazine* as featured celebrity residents. Kids from the neighborhood would come to knock on the door for an autograph or to wish Greg good luck with the new season. I remember constantly feeling it was all too good to be true and wondered when someone would jump out from behind an imaginary curtain and yell, "You have been punked! Greg ran off with Christy Brinkley and your old job washing hair is waiting for you. Show is over!"

It was opening day at the Astrodome, and I could hardly contain my excitement for the game. It all felt very surreal as I was guided down the stairs to the family section of the stadium. For a moment, I suddenly felt as if I did not belong. For one thing, my clothes were all wrong, as I realized I was very under dressed. Neiman Marcus quickly became my preferred place to shop with the help of the kind and enthusiastic salesladies. They were more than happy to load up my dressing room with presentable clothing, thanks to my limitless new credit card. My old wardrobe had consisted of black pants and t-shirts for work, Western clothes for when I went dancing three nights a week, and a couple of nice dresses. I also had Rocky Mountain jeans and Justin Roper boots in every color. And right now you are laughing if you know what those jeans are, they were the Gloria Vanderbilts of the Western world.

Back then, wives dressed up for games from head to toe, and my closet was stocked with all the things needed to be an official big league baseball wife. I tried to learn as much about baseball, and most importantly, pitching, as I could. Greg would tell me what all the stats on the back of his baseball cards meant and what the difference was between a good ERA and a bad one. It was a whole new world, and I needed to learn the language fast.

As the season went on, I started to feel more and more at home at the ballpark. I had formed close friendships with many of the other wives. Unfortunately, there were the few "mean girl" wives who were not very nice, especially to a new young wife or girlfriend. I really never understood it, because at one time they were the new girl. There was one veteran wife in particular who seemed to enjoy picking and choosing who she was going to let in to her friend zone and whose life she would make as uncomfortable as possible. You would think grown women on the same team would treat each other nicely, but that was not always the case. At times it felt like I was right back in high school, dealing with a bully who had no reason to dislike me other than the fact I was new and young. When word got out I was writing this book, I had several wives contact me, asking me to please write about some of the women who were so rough on some of us, and I learned I was not alone. While I will never mention names, I am sure they will know exactly who they are. Hopefully, now they are a much better version of who they used to be.

I also quickly learned baseball can be unforgiving at times, with the "What have you done for me lately" pressure. The press and fans loved the players who were on a hot streak and producing numbers, rightfully so. But when a player was struggling for one reason or another, they would be ripped to shreds, especially by a sports writer. Greg had a bit of a rocky start with the Astros and the press was brutal at times, even talking about his weight being an issue. I know it got to him, and it got to me even more. He had been in the big leagues for seven years at this point and knew about all the ups and downs of the sport.

He would always tell me, "Sarah, you have to take the good with the bad."

But I would still get so unsettled when people bad-mouthed him after a rough outing. It was especially difficult sitting in the stands when things weren't going his way, having to listen to people boo and say horrible things out loud within my earshot. It took everything I had to not stand up and tell them to go throw a little ball into a tiny box in front of thirty thousand people as they are yelling at you. It got better with time, but it was definitely hard getting used to. My heart broke for Greg when he didn't pitch well, but he always managed to shake it off and go out again five days later with the same positive attitude. To this very day, Greg and I often look back on those days when he would tell me to "Take the good with the bad." We would refer back to that simple statement many times over the years to come.

During our three and a half years with the Astros, life was filled with so many incredible moments that girls my age could only dream about. I was crazy, madly in love, and Greg loved to spoil me whenever he could. He is a huge gift-giver and loved adorning me with beautiful jewelry, cars and clothes, no reason or special occasion needed. Once, he gave me a diamond tennis bracelet in the middle of the cereal section at a grocery store, just because he couldn't wait one minute longer. Another time, right before a game was about to start in San Diego, he motioned me down to the dugout from where I was sitting in the stands. I could feel the curious eyes of fans watching for what was about to happen as I approached Greg, who always looked so good to me in uniform. He took my hand and placed a gorgeous sapphire and diamond ring in my palm. Again, just because. I will just say Tiffany should have been my middle name for a while, as I had more little blue boxes in my closet than I could count. After I had my third child, he picked me up from the hospital in a brand-new black Mercedes as my "push present" and I had to wonder what would have happened if I'd had twins!

Greg not only loved to give things but was also a true romantic. He has the ability to make you feel as if you are the most amazing person in the world, which would surprise a lot of people because he is so quiet. He wrote beautiful cards and would always leave sweet little love notes around the house. He once wrote me a poem on a bunch of airline napkins. I still have it tucked away in a special place, along with the piles of cards I keep in a memory box.

Hayley was four years old and thriving in her new magical world. She soon started calling Greg, or Gweg as she would pronounce it, "Daddy," which melted his heart. Hayley rarely saw Sean, and the few times she did, she would cry to come home the moment she arrived at Sean's trailer in New Mexico. This went on for years and was extremely hard on Hayley. At such a young age, she wasn't able to comprehend why she had to make these visits. We tried to explain how important it was, but visiting a man she hardly knew was obviously difficult for her to understand. There were tearful and painful goodbyes as she begged us not to make her go. It tore my heart out to see her so upset. Even though Sean was her father, it was a vastly different world for her.

I found myself making up excuse after excuse not to send her, but eventually Sean took us to court to force visitation despite the fact he had never paid child support. He won, and the visits resumed, even after Hayley told the court she didn't want to go. I clearly remember watching Sean struggle to get Hayley into his rental car as her arms reached toward me, begging and crying not to go. It was heartbreaking for both of us, as we had no choice in the matter. Finally, Sean stopped forcing the visits, and they rarely spoke again until many years later; even that didn't last long.

Even after Hayley had initiated contact again later in her teens, Sean and his parents stopped responding to her. Looking back, I wonder if it was my fault she had to go through all that pain and confusion, because I was the one who chose to move so far away when she was so young. This is something I will always feel bad about. I wonder what would the outcome have been if I had forced the visitation issue, or not moved at all. Would they have had a better relationship? We have these same painful thoughts about Greg's daughter. A true sliding-doors scenario we will never have the answer to.

Sean and his family had no reason to stop all communication, especially once Hayley tried to reconnect years later. It was their choice, not ours. I think because Hayley and I have always been so close, having to leave me for an extended period of time was just too much for her, as it would be for any young child. I think she didn't want to miss a single minute with her new expanding family, and she was about to become a big sister.

Greg and I wanted a baby as soon as possible after we got married and quickly became pregnant. About two months into the pregnancy, I suddenly started bleeding heavily and later miscarried. We were both devastated—this was the first real-life setback we experienced together. However, two months later I got pregnant again. I was more careful this time not to celebrate too early, or tell very many people, just in case. After the third month, I felt I could breathe a little sigh of relief and get excited about the life growing inside me. At almost four months along, I started to show and wore my little bump with pride, glowing with excitement.

At a routine doctor's appointment, Greg and I were joking around as usual as the ultrasound technician started to navigate over my belly. We both noticed a look of concern form on her face and immediately knew something was wrong. I briefly thought, "Oh no! Twins?" It was when she asked to be excused to get the doctor that I got scared. The doctor came in and started the exam again. He was silent for a moment. That's when I figured it out, before he even said a word. I didn't hear the little heartbeat that had been so strong the month before.

"I'm so sorry," the doctor said solemnly. "The baby is no longer viable. You can wait for it to pass on its own, but I suggest a D&C. It will be much less traumatic than waiting for nature to take its course."

A D&C is not an easy procedure, and a very emotional one. The baby I already loved so much was going to have to be removed surgically. It was only a few minutes ago that we were laughing and joking around, excited to hear our baby's beating heart and to see how much it had grown since last month.

I felt like I was hit by a truck and started quietly crying. Greg was fighting back his own tears as he held my hand. I let it all out when the doctor stepped out of the room. I was sobbing and could not believe it was happening all over again when I was so far along. I finally got myself together and we started to leave the exam room, then something happened that I will never forget.

One of the nurses came up to us with a shy smile and said, "I know this is a bad time, but could I please have your autograph?" We had just been told our baby was dead, and she wanted Greg's autograph.

"Are you freaking serious?" he barked back. Not waiting for a response, we walked out of the building, and Greg held me as we both cried for the baby we would never meet.

Thankfully, two months later I was pregnant once again. This pregnancy was smooth sailing, and I didn't have an ounce of trouble. I absolutely loved being pregnant and all the magic that comes along with growing a human in your belly. The bigger my belly got, the more beautiful I felt; and if it was up to me, I would stay barefoot and pregnant.

Brenna Katelyn was born October 27, 1994, after a flawless delivery, and was a perfect little seven-pound beauty with a hearty cry to announce her arrival. I watched Greg hold her with such pride after they had cleaned her off and wrapped her tightly in the striped pink and blue blanket and little hat. She looked so tiny in his strong arms as he kept saying over and over again how much he loved us. My heart was filled with so much love, I thought I might burst.

The off-season had just begun, and I was over-the-moon happy with my growing little family. I loved that Greg was home for a while to enjoy the kids, and he was an amazing help with middle-of-the-night feedings and diaper changes. Hayley was thrilled to finally have a baby sister, and Brenna hardly left her side. Things were certainly a little more hectic now with two children, but I loved it. I was incredibly happy and filled with an enormous sense of contentment and gratitude.

ABOUT HALFWAY INTO THE second season with the Astros, I quickly learned more about another side of professional sports. Infidelity was all around me. It was the sort of a thing that if you saw it happening, you just kept your mouth shut. If one of the wives decided to travel to the city where the team was playing, there were silent rules she needed to honor, like not going to the hotel bar after games to make sure she didn't walk in on something she should not see. Many times I would accidentally see a player with someone other than his wife in the hotel lobby, sitting in the bar, or walking around the city. I would just smile and turn away.

Girls would hang around the hotel with a look about them that clearly shouted, "I'm here to snag me a baseball player!"

One time, a scantily dressed blonde came up to me and a few other wives sitting in the stands and started asking if we knew where the family section was. She informed us that a certain player had left her a ticket. That certain player's wife was sitting right next to me and firmly let that girl know it.

It was just the culture to look away, to act like it was not your problem or your place to say anything. The first year into my own marriage, girls would call the hotel asking for Greg, not realizing he was married and that I was there in the room. Greg was no angel before me, but I know without a doubt that he was faithful to me his entire career.

While I saw it happen on every team he played for, there were many more good guys than bad; guys who loved their wives and were stellar human beings. Most of these guys gave generously to charities, visited sick children in hospitals, and worked hard to be the best they could be. On and off the field, they were role models to so many. Many of these retired players and their wives are still going strong, not part of the high divorce rate that plagues professional athletes. But I do understand how it all happens. Money and fame coming at such an early age can be a deadly combination to a young couple. I think this holds true outside of professional sports as well. Coming into such extreme amounts of money can give a false sense of "I can get away with anything I want," no matter at what age it happens.

I recently had a glass of wine with a couple of friends from the baseball days. We talked about how new players and their wives should receive some kind of guidance, even therapy, to deal with all the challenges they have no idea are coming their way. Being armed with knowledge ahead of time could save countless families from the devastating consequences that can develop from that lifestyle.

On April 8, 1996, we welcomed Sophia Forest to our ever-growing family. She, too, was an easy delivery, perfect from head to toe and our first little blonde baby. Greg had the Astros game on TV during the entire delivery, and up until my three pushes, I was watching right along with him. I was only twenty-seven, and even though I was still young, I felt incredibly blessed and content with our three perfect daughters. I decided I was done with having children and had my tubes tied while I was in the hospital. Just like that, our family of five was complete.

While life at home was everything I could ever wish for, Greg continued to struggle professionally with the Astros. Looking back, those numbers would be considered mega-millions-worthy in today's terms, but I am sure the guys playing ten years before him felt the same way. Ultimately, in the third year of his four-year contract, the Astros decided to release him. I knew he was devastated, but with his calm demeanor he never let it show. It had to have felt like a punch in the gut, and my heart hurt for him. The team and the city he loved so much didn't think he was worth it anymore.

I clearly remember feeling like it was the end of the world for us all. I'm sure I was very dramatic about the whole thing. It also didn't help that I was having a little postpartum depression, as I struggled with it for a short time with each baby. I knew we were going to be fine financially, but you just never know exactly when your career is over in baseball. Greg was only twenty-nine years old and out of a job halfway through the season. It was time for me to wake up and realize that things can't always be as easy and glamorous as I'd gotten used to. We just had to wait and hope that another team would pick him up, and thankfully, one did.

The Cleveland Indians signed Greg for the remainder of the 1996 season. He had started his career there ten years earlier, and he was excited to get back to the city where it all started for him. Me? I was not as excited that our home life was about to be flipped upside down. I was still trying to get acclimated to being a mother of three, not to mention a newborn. We ended up living in a hotel for a month in Cleveland since the season was close to being over. There was no such thing as Airbnb or HomeAway back then, so options were slim. Thankfully, I was fortunate enough to have a nanny and my parents come with us. It was so nice to have other adults with me while Greg was at the ballpark or traveling with the team. I can't begin to imagine what the hotel bill was for our suite plus two other rooms for that month, but I'm sure it was a crazy amount that would probably give me a heart attack now.

Living in a beautiful hotel for a while with a free cocktail hour every day at five o'clock, room service whenever you wanted, within walking distance to all the shops and restaurants in downtown Cleveland sounds like a dream come true to me now. At the time, I thought it was the most traumatic thing in the world. Granted, I had three small kids with me 24/7, but I also had a babysitter and my parents to help me out. Sometimes I just have to shake my head at the things that got me so stressed out back then. My twenty-seven-year-old spoiled brain just didn't get it. Looking back, I have to say it was pretty damn fun. If you ask Hayley, living in that hotel might be one of the top ten favorite memories from her childhood. She still talks about piling her little plastic plate high with endless cheese and cracker choices and her Shirley Temples, always with three cherries.

Greg's second time around with the Indians was not nearly as stellar as the first. I could see he was actually starting to doubt himself and his abilities. It was hard to know what to say or do to make him feel better. Even though I was busy enough with the kids and mommy stuff to keep me occupied, I was nervous about what was next for our family. Was he done? Would another team sign him? He was still young, but newer talent was constantly showing up, knocking the older guys off the block.

We were both glad when the season ended. We were so ready to go home to Houston and just enjoy three months off with no stress about what was happening next in the unpredictable world of baseball. The last year had taken a mental toll on him. He was ready for a much-needed break, and we were ready to have Daddy around. I was tired of living out of a suitcase, juggling children in a city I never truly felt comfortable in, for a team that really didn't seem to want us there.

During the off-season in 1997, Greg was offered a small contract with the Minnesota Twins. Okay, small in the baseball salary world, but we were grateful and excited that they were giving him a shot. I had never been to Minnesota, but I was no stranger to the long-distance lifestyle by this point in our marriage. I stayed in Houston until summer so Hayley could finish school. The three months apart was brutal, but if you need a little spice in your marriage, the long-distance thing will do it. When I was able to go and visit Greg, we were like wild teenagers. Thanks to my parents coming to stay with the kids, I could travel to wherever the team was playing all over the United States. Sometimes I would be waiting in the hotel room when he came in after a game, with something sexy on, sprawled on the bed with room service and wine.

If I got to the city before the game started, I would go to the stadium, and he would always be able to pick me out in the stands, waving at me vivaciously without caring what the other guys thought. We would walk hand in hand in cities like New York, San Diego, Los Angeles, Boston and Atlanta, shopping without ever even looking at price tags. Spending thousands in a day was nothing to us. We were, no doubt, living large, loving life, and loving each other.

Some teams let the wives fly with the players on their charter planes, which was really exciting. I loved seeing the real personalities of the players off the field. We would laugh nonstop on those flights. One of the guys loved to stand in the aisle of the plane as it was taking off, with his hands out like a bird, sunglasses on and scarf wrapped around his neck as if in mid-flight on a ski jump. He called himself "Eddie the Eagle," and he did this on every single takeoff as the plane climbed into the sky. Greg and I would bring mini versions of the games we loved to play at home on the plane, like *Yahtzee* and *Scrabble*. We were quickly nicknamed "The Hasbros" by one of the players. Wine, beer and cocktails were plentiful on each flight, and trays filled with snacks would be passed around by flight attendants lucky enough to work those flights. I could see the brotherhood the guys had with each other, as they were family for eight months out of the year. I guess you could say we were all a family.

I think most people don't realize that baseball wives are single mothers eight months out of the year. We handle everything from caring for the children, paying bills, carpools, playdates, doctor visits, school registrations, car issues, to organizing and planning a move to a totally different state at the last minute after a trade. I do have to say that when Greg was home, he attended every single kid activity, got up with the babies, helped with meals and took kids to and from school. He was always enthusiastically involved with the family during the off-seasons. As much as I enjoyed the baseball season, the off-season was always my favorite time, because we were a whole family, and I was not the single mom in charge of, quite literally, everything.

Trust me, I do realize how incredibly lucky I was to be able to have the resources to hire a housekeeper and a babysitter during the baseball years. I remember thinking it was so hard doing it alone. And, yes, it was hard at times, but I usually had someone around to help during the day. I was so fortunate compared to so many other *real* single mamas out there, who didn't have the luxury of hiring help and unlimited funds to ease the stress of being alone all the time. I realize how lucky I was, and I have so much respect for moms who are truly going it alone for whatever reason, especially military spouses. Those women (and men!) are true heros.

In Minnesota, Greg's career hit a major turnaround. He was back, no longer as a starter, but as a reliever and left-handed specialist. He found a new role and he was good at it. This would end up extending his career for many years to come. After almost two outstanding seasons with the Twins, I got a call from Greg one evening that I was not prepared for.

"Sarah, I have just been traded to the Boston Red Sox, and I have to leave tonight."

I was in my hotel room packing my suitcase to head back to Houston after a three-day visit with Greg when I got the call. I had grown to love the Twins organization and all the wives on the team, and the girls loved being there as well. Even though I was only there in the summer full-time with the kids and during small visits when I could get away, they had become family.

I now had to fly back to Minnesota to pack up our rental house and organize getting all of our things home to Houston. Breaking the news to our girls was not an easy conversation, either.

"Mommy, can the Red Sox please ask Samantha's daddy to come too so we can still play together?" Hayley asked with her sweet innocence.

"No, sweetie, Sam's daddy has to stay and help the Twins for the next two years, but we will make new friends on the new team just like we always do!" I explained, choking back my own tears.

Brenna and Sophia were still too young to really understand that we probably would not be seeing the friends they had made on the Twins, unless we ended up being on the same team somewhere else down the road. They knew that every team had a family room with lots of kids to make friends with, no matter where we were, and it made all the transitions a bit easier.

It was time to collect myself and remember that it was a very exciting event for Greg. This would be the first chance in his career to make it to postseason play. The Boston Red Sox needed his help in the bullpen to win the Wild Card Division. The Sox did end up winning the Wild Card; however, that was as far as they would advance that season. Greg got a taste of what the road to the World Series was like, and he was hungry for more. The 1998 baseball season had come to an exciting end for Greg and a very tiring end for me.

The kids were getting more and more active and could be a real handful for me at times, especially with all the travel back and forth to and from Minnesota those last couple of seasons. Yes, I was that poor woman on the plane no one ever wanted to sit near with three little ones in tow. Especially because two of them always seemed to get airsick. Thankfully, it was usually just before landing, and I quickly learned to have extra clothes handy in my oversized purse—not in the overhead bin, I had learned the hard way one very eventful and messy landing.

Our home base was still in Houston, Texas, and I was there with the kids while Greg finished the season with the Red Sox. He was about to become a free agent since he was at the end of his contract, meaning he was eligible to freely sign with any team that was interested in him. He was coming off two great years as a relief pitcher, and good lefties were in high demand. I could tell Greg was in a much better place mentally after making it through those humbling years. It seemed his career was in a rebirth in a way, now that his days as a starting pitcher were over.

I still had a place in my heart for Arizona from my brief time at Arizona State, and Greg loved the time he spent there during spring training. I loved the vibrant sunsets in the fall, the mountains sprinkled with cactus, and the thunderous monsoon storms in the summer. The Arizona Diamondbacks were a brand-new team in the Phoenix area and had only been in existence for one year at that time. One day over the phone I casually asked him, "What do you think about making a move to Arizona when you're done and try to get on the new team there?"

With a hint of excitement and zero hesitation, he said, "That's all you had to say."

The girls were almost ten, four, and three when we told them the news that we were leaving Texas for good once Daddy was done in Boston. They all squealed with excitement, and Brenna shouted, "I can't wait to touch a cactus!" Sophia danced around with her beloved pacifier in her mouth, mimicking her older sisters, who were dancing with joy upon hearing the news.

While we were sad to leave both of our families in Houston, we were excited for our new Arizona adventure. The girls were getting older, and we wanted to stay in one city where we could have Dad around during the season when the team was playing home games. Greg would still be gone half the time, but that also meant he would be home half the time. Brenna would be starting kindergarten soon, and she was blossoming into a smart and, at times, very sassy little lady. She would strike up conversations with just about anyone, from a server at a restaurant, to the attendant at the car wash, which was her favorite place to go. She would explode with joy when Greg would announce he was going. "Chips? Candy? Diet Coke? I LOVE the car wash!" she would exclaim, jumping into Greg's arms. Brenna was my strong-willed child. She enjoyed testing me more than the other girls did and brought me to tears of frustration more than once. But her fierce independence was so much more of an asset than a liability and would come in very handy later in her life. She was the child who would stick up for anyone who was being mistreated, loved every kind of animal, and was always very keenly aware of everything going on around her. One thing is for certain: She was 100 percent a daddy's girl.

Hayley was the classic oldest child, with a constant need to please everyone, especially me. She was, and still is, one of the kindest young ladies I know, and by far the most sensitive of our three girls, especially during her younger years. She never got into any trouble and was a very strict rule follower. She loved Brenna and Sophia and was the perfect playmate; she made up games, created dance productions for Greg and me to giggle through, and was my little shadow. If Dad was out of town, she always slept in bed with me, her little arm snuggly wrapped around mine. Hayley and I are more like sisters than mother and daughter. Maybe it's because I had her so young, but mostly because she is so easy to talk to, laugh with and gives the best advice. I sure needed a lot of that through the years.

Sophia was my sweet and spunky little blondie. She had baby-fine hair that stuck straight up until she was four years old. It reminded me of Tweety Bird. She also was sensitive, did not like getting in trouble, was the most creative, and had the biggest imagination. She was the child who would be happy alone in her room, coloring or playing with her dolls while her sisters were off doing something else. I will say she could throw some serious tantrums if she was overtired or *really* wanted something; like the red, sparkly shoes I refused to get her at Target one day. I'm not exactly sure, but we might still be banned from that particular store. She has the best sense of humor, and no one can make me cry with laughter more than she can.

One thing I can say about these amazing daughters of mine, is that from the time they were tiny little ones, to now being grown women, their individual personalities have not changed all that much. Through all the challenges that tested the three of them in various and sometimes terrifying ways, they have stayed much the same, true to their own beautiful and unique qualities.

Being the home-finding expert that I am, I found the perfect house in Paradise Valley, Arizona, in just one day. My dear friend and the wife of one of the Minnesota Twins, flew to Arizona with me to house-hunt while Greg was still in Boston. Even now, that house is still a Swindell favorite. It was the centerpiece to three of the best years of our lives, the house we lived in the longest, and the one we wished we had never sold. It was a rambling, one-story Southwest-style home that surrounded a huge pool with a waterfall, a koi pond and citrus trees. Every home in the neighborhood sat on an acre lot, so we had lots of privacy and space for the kids to play, and it was walking distance to the elementary school. It was a tad out of our budget, but I fell in love with it the moment I saw it. I took a video of it with my camcorder and showed it to Greg on a quick trip to Boston for a playoff game.

"Looks like a winner, I love it!" he said after watching the tiny screen on the camcorder.

A few weeks later, with the help of my parents, we packed up our Texas home and moved to Arizona. I worked to get the house all ready for Greg when he came home after that final heartbreaking playoff loss with Boston. I was sad the team lost, but beyond happy that my husband was coming home to enjoy a relaxing off-season in our new paradise. When he walked through the door, he could not believe how beautiful the house was. I have to laugh a little that we bought the house without Greg seeing it first, but I laugh even more because it started a trend.

Our prayers were soon answered, and during that off-season, Greg signed a contract with the Arizona Diamondbacks. Everything was falling perfectly into place, almost too perfectly.

Greg's career was going well the first year with the D-backs, and all of the girls were thriving in their new environment. Within a year, the team was stocked with veteran players hungry for a World Series title, which seemed far-fetched, considering they were such a new team. But the chemistry between the players was undeniable, and the city was buzzing with excitement. All of the players were having their own exceptionally good year. It was like the perfect storm—something amazing was about to happen, we all felt it, the entire city felt it.

I loved being back in Arizona with all the beautiful sunshine-filled days. It was hot, of course, but a totally different kind of heat. It was much more bearable than Houston's humidity. I was also getting to dabble a little into my dream of being in front of the camera. I was asked to be a regular guest correspondent for the *D-backs Playin' Hardball*, a post-game show on TV. I did seven or eight episodes interviewing players' wives in their homes, as well as segments in ballparks around the United States, speaking with fans in the stands. Sometimes our family would be featured on the show. They would follow us around our house with a camera, capturing a typical day in our lives. We were reality TV before it ever became a thing!

I was also getting back into modeling, doing commercial print work with the Ford Agency. I was literally living my childhood dreams, just in a different order than I had originally planned, and loving every minute of it. I was extremely busy, but with help, I happily juggled all of it. I felt like the luckiest girl in the world to have such an amazing life. I was so grateful for everything, especially my beautiful family that I loved with all my heart.

One night during the off-season, I had a crazy dream that I had a baby boy. With Sophia now three years old, I was having a severe case of baby fever. I ended up deciding to have surgery to untie my tubes. The doctors were able to repair one of my tubes, making it possible for me to get pregnant every other month. Just like a gremlin, you throw water on me and I multiply. When we got the news that we were having a boy, Greg could not contain his tears. I vividly remember the ultrasound technician saying, "Yep, I see a boy part!" It was incredible: We were finally going to have a son who would complete our family perfectly. Greg was proud that the Swindell name would continue on with our new little addition on the way.

I was sailing right along with the pregnancy, busy getting ready to be a mother of four while the Diamondbacks were leading the pack in their division. Then, out of the blue at thirty-six weeks, I started having real contractions that did not stop. It was too early, so I was admitted to the hospital and given medication to try and stop the labor. The medication made me so sick to my stomach, I vomited violently, which made my water break. There was no turning back once that happened; Dawson was coming early, ready or not. As usual, Greg and I were joking around in the hospital, filming ourselves and being silly once the nausea had subsided and the epidural worked its magic. *D-Backs Playin' Hardball* even did a post-game segment on our son's birth using some of our own family footage, giving baseball fans an intimate peek into our sometimes wacky sense of humor.

We were hopeful all would be okay, since the baby weighed almost seven pounds, according to the ultrasound. On February 4th, 2001, Dawson Harold was born. But his delivery was very different from the other three, and the joyous moment after your baby is born, when the nurse places your newborn on your chest, lasted only a minute or so.

He immediately had trouble breathing, as his lungs had not yet fully developed, even though his size suggested otherwise. Within minutes, the nurses took Dawson from my arms with an unexpected urgency in their worried eyes.

I remember Greg looking very nervous. He hovered around the clear plastic bassinet as the nurse dutifully checked Dawson's vitals. The pediatrician on-call came in to look at him and immediately said he needed to go to the NICU. It happened so fast, my legs were still in the stirrups as the nurse hurried Dawson out of my sight, while my heart broke in two.

A few hours later, he was airlifted to a Level 1 hospital equipped to handle high-risk premature babies. Just before he was transported, they brought him into my room, and I was finally able to really see my son for the first time since his birth. It's crazy because he looked so perfect. He wasn't even that small, but he struggled to breathe the minute they took him from under the oxygen hood. I kissed him on his tiny forehead as they took him from my arms once more, off to the waiting helicopter.

My heart shattered having to let him go. I was panicked that I might never see him again. Tears poured down my face as I heard the helicopter outside my hospital window take off. The next morning I was well enough to join him at the other hospital. I could not wait to see him again. I have to admit, Dawson was nothing like the other tiny premature babies. He looked like a mini Sumo wrestler in comparison to the tiny three-pound girl in the incubator next to him. After just five days, Dawson was ready to come home and was doing remarkably well. I felt like we had dodged a life-changing bullet and was grateful beyond words to be taking our little boy home to his eagerly waiting sisters.

Life was slowly getting back to normal, and I was getting used to all the craziness that having four children brings to a household. Luckily, I found the most amazing lady in the world to help me out while Greg was gone. I hate to use the word "nanny" or "housekeeper," because she was so much more than that. Maria was a part of our family, as were her two children. Without her, I would have lost my mind many times during the days when Greg was on the road. She was the kindest, most loving person in the world, and best of all, she loved my children as her own. Maria, her husband and her kids were part of our family for many years, and we still stay in touch. My parents, especially my mom, were also pivotal for my mental survival. They stayed with the kids many times so I could meet Greg on the road.

The Diamondbacks were on fire and had won the National League Championship in only their fourth year of existence. For many of the veteran players, Greg included, it would be their first shot at a World Series title. It was a magical team that year, and something special was brewing in that locker room.

Then it happened: September 11, 2001, America was attacked. Everything stopped, including baseball.

Greg came in the door from dropping the kids off at school and said, "Shit is going down, babe!"

At first I thought he was talking about the new landscapers working at the house, but when he turned on the TV, I knew it was far from that.

Suddenly, nothing mattered anymore, especially something as frivolous as a baseball game or a World Series title. America held its collective breath for a long time, as we tried to figure out how something so horrific could happen, and how on earth were we supposed to go on living life as if it hadn't. After about a month, the country slowly started getting back to normal, whatever that was going to look like. The new normal included baseball. People were hungry for the return of America's favorite pastime. It was like we wanted to hold America as high up as possible for the world to see—we were not broken, and we would show what our country stood for.

The New York Yankees and the Arizona Diamondbacks played in the World Series one month after the attacks. We easily won the first two out of seven games at home, and were going to New York to play baseball, as the Twin Towers were still smoldering and the city was still grieving. To try and describe what it was like to ride the team bus to the field for Game 3 is almost impossible and certainly a chill-bump-worthy moment. The wives, significant others and family members rode together in several charter buses to Yankee Stadium. My brothers, who were as awestruck as I was, had flown in to join me. I left the children at home with my mom and Maria for fear there would be another attack, as President George W. Bush would be throwing out the first pitch, and rumors were flying. I almost didn't go to New York myself, but I knew this might be the last chance for Greg to be in a World Series, and I wouldn't miss this dream come true. But the decision to go and leave the kids at home scared me, and I struggled with it as I rode the bus in. Many of the wives struggled with the same thoughts about their own children, but we tried to put it out of our minds as best we could to focus on the excitement around us.

I don't recall how many police cars and motorcycles escorted our bus to Yankee Stadium from our Manhattan hotel, but there were a lot. People on the streets lined up, cheering with homemade signs. There was an undeniable feeling that even though we were competing against each other, we were one big family.

When President George W. Bush slowly and confidently walked to the mound, the stadium roared with applause. There was no holding back the tears. Everyone cried at the sight of our brave President, clearly risking his own life by being in the most vulnerable position a man could be in so soon after we were attacked. There was not a dry eye in the stadium as the National Anthem played; even the players were wiping away tears. So much emotion filled that stadium that you could almost taste it.

Sitting in the stands for those three games felt like a dream, with an energy that can never be duplicated. For Game 5, the last of the three games we played in New York, my brothers and I sat way at the top of Yankee Stadium because there was an overflow of tickets needed in the family section. We volunteered to take the seats up on top along with a few other Diamondback families, thinking a little superstitiously that it may bring some luck after losing two straight games. We were surrounded by Yankees fans who playfully, yet loudly, let us know we were in their territory, and we loved it. We could literally feel the stadium rock from side to side from the fans jumping up and down with each hit our pitcher gave up.

Our games in New York didn't go quite as planned, and all three were lost in heartbreaking finishes. Since we had won the first two at home, it was time for the best out of seven to be finished back in Arizona. Greg had pitched a couple of times by this point, and his outings went perfectly. To see him on the mound, living the dream he'd had since he was a little boy, was incredible and such an honor to share with him. Even though I felt physically ill with nerves watching him on the field, there is nothing sexier than watching your husband pitch in the World Series. Then again, he made my heart pound just entering a room.

I will never forget the look on his face when he stepped onto the mound in Yankee Stadium. He stood there with a tiny smile and a look of pure amazement as he soaked in all that was happening around him. It was as if he never wanted that moment to end. It was the moment almost every little boy dreams of.

They won Game 6 at home in a blowout. Game 7, the final game, was the next evening, and the energy at Bank One Ballpark was almost mystical. White rally towels filled the stadium as fans vigorously twirled them to the sound of thumping music. Fighter jets whizzed by the opened-roofed stadium just before the first pitch, as chills covered my entire body. I will never forget that moment. The whole city of Phoenix felt like one giant family. I don't think Greg slept a wink the night before Game 7. Knowing the end of his career was probably coming soon, this career highlight could not have come at a better time, or with better teammates than the ones who filled the 2001 roster.

It was a close game through eight innings, but it was not looking good going into the ninth. We were a few runs behind, and the Yankees' best closer, Mariano Rivera, was on the mound. Just as all the wives had started talking about what a great year it had been and how the boys should still be so proud, there was a sudden shift in the game.

Just when we thought it was all over, a bloop single by Luis Gonzalez into shallow center sent the winning run home, and the stadium erupted in pandemonium. Only a few short minutes had passed between anticipating a loss, to jumping around frantically, hugging everyone and crying with joy that they had won! Fans were embracing and kissing complete strangers. There probably was not a dry eye in the whole state of Arizona.

Wives and family members rushed down the stands, trying not to fall over one another to get on the field. I have never seen more grown men crying than I did once I got down there. When I finally found him, he wept as we hugged tighter than we ever had. His life's dream had finally come true, after almost seventeen years in the big leagues. I was honored to be right beside him, sharing his incredible moment. To this day, it is one of the most epic World Series comebacks in baseball history, when the Diamondbacks came back to win it all and beat Mariano Rivera. We beat the New York Yankees!

A few days later we were riding on top of fire trucks through downtown Phoenix in the biggest ticker tape parade I had ever seen—another top lifetime moment I will never forget. Seeing the complete awe in my children's faces as we rode through downtown, confetti falling all around us, was pure magic. Their wide eyes seeing all the fans in the streets cheering and clapping for *us* is something they will never forget.

Not long after the parade, the entire team, staff and their significant others were flown to Washington, D.C., to meet President Bush in the White House. Walking the long white corridor of the White House to shake the hand of our President was the perfect ending to an already unbelievable dream.

The kids were suddenly stars at school, now that their dad was part of the World Series Champion Team.

"Mom! Someone wanted *my* autograph today!" Hayley exclaimed as she ran in the door one day after school.

Brenna and Sophia basked in all their new popularity as well. While kids at school already thought they were cool because their dad was a pro baseball player, this launched them all into a whole new stratosphere of coolness, and they loved it. I did have a nagging sting of sadness about it, though. Dawson wasn't aware of all the excitement since he was still just a baby. He was sick with a terrible ear infection on the day of the parade, and we thought it would be best to not bring him. I knew we could rely on videos and pictures when he was old enough, and he would be so proud of his dad. Maybe that would even be Dawson one day, living the same dream as a pitcher in the big leagues, just like his daddy.

Winning the 2001 World Series was an almost eerie finale to our *Wonder Years*. We didn't realize at the time just how drastically our lives were about to change, how much our marriage would be tested, and how our family would never be the same again.

AFTER THE EXCITEMENT OF THE World Series win had settled down, we happily got back to normal. We were all anxious to have Dad home for a relaxing three-month off-season. The girls were happy and healthy, but Dawson struggled with ear infection after ear infection. He was almost a year old and had been on one antibiotic after another. The medications just couldn't seem to knock out the ear infections and nagging upper respiratory issue he was having. Other than being sick a lot, he was a happy boy and hitting most of his milestones after his rocky start at life.

In early February, Greg left for spring training, just after Dawson's first birthday. Saying goodbye was always difficult, as it marked the beginning of single parenthood for me once again. We always had a tearful farewell, and as always, Greg gave me a beautifully written card and Valentine's Day gift before he left. It was getting harder and harder to travel with four children, so we rarely made the trip to Tucson during the six weeks of spring training anymore, which made the goodbyes even more emotional.

I was starting to get a bit concerned that Dawson was not even close to walking, and he started crawling later than normal. His pediatrician told us that since he was six weeks early, it was not unusual. He was a chunky kid, and I wondered if his extra weight was holding him back, so I resolved to be more patient and less worried.

His pediatrician suggested physical therapy after he turned fifteen months to get the ball rolling for his walking. I remember being almost embarrassed at the thought of physical therapy, connecting it to kids with real disabilities. I had visions of kids in wheelchairs and walkers. He was just chubby and a little behind, not disabled!

It started to seem like Dawson was sick all the time. He was having diarrhea constantly, in addition to the ear infections and respiratory problems. At his well-baby checkup shortly before he turned fifteen months, it was time for a round of shots. He was still on antibiotics from his previous ear infection, and I was concerned that he might not be well enough to handle the round of vaccinations. I was anxious to ask the doctor about it.

The possible connection between vaccines and autism was just starting to be a serious topic among new moms, and I immediately thought about all the whispers going around about this very touchy topic. I had always been pro-vaccine. I believed a parent who didn't follow the strict guidelines and recommendations of their pediatrician was being irresponsible. Just a few days earlier, my neighbor Janice and I were chatting in the driveway with our babies in tow, when she told me she was going to delay her son's shots for a while, just to be safe. At the time, I wasn't in the mood to get into a vaccine debate while standing in the scorching Arizona heat, so I listened patiently for a while, not really absorbing what she said.

"I hear what you're saying, my friend. But just think if everyone stopped vaccinating, wouldn't we all be in worse trouble?" I asked, wiping the thin layer of sweat that was forming on my forehead.

"I'm not saying that I won't get him vaccinated, I just want to do it at a slower pace. It feels like too many at once, if you really think about it," Janice explained.

## Chapter 8

As I stood waiting in the doctor's office, with a very fussy Dawson on my hip, that conversation crept into my head. Could she be right? This strange and wise voice inside me, the one I have now learned NEVER to ignore, whispered in my ear: *stop, stop!*

That voice said, "Do not sign that consent, take your baby home and wait." I didn't listen.

Instead, I looked the nurse in the eye and asked if she was sure it was okay to give Dawson the round of shots after he had been sick for so long. She assured me all was fine since he did not have a fever, and his ears and chest were clear.

I thought, *What do I know? I am not a doctor, I didn't go to medical school, I haven't read the latest medical journals. Surely they would never give anything to a baby that could cause harm.*

As I signed the form, I felt a feeling of panic run through my body, and I silently prayed that I was doing the right thing. I quickly convinced myself that I was a good mother for listening to the nurse and that I was protecting my son from all the deadly diseases apparently floating all over Arizona that would surely kill him if I didn't. The nurse told me to just give him Tylenol when we got home if he seemed fussy, and she sent us on our way.

The next morning when I went into Dawson's room to get him from his crib, I noticed a small amount of vomit on his mattress. He was getting sick yet again. My first thought was that the ear infection had come back. I honestly didn't even consider it might be a reaction from the vaccine. I am not sure if it was because I was busy getting the girls ready for school, or if I had subconsciously stuffed the possibility way down deep inside. *Dawson was just getting sick again, it was nothing more than that,* I thought, as I tended to the girls.

I was set to leave town two days later to meet up with Greg. Trying to go anywhere for more than a day with four young children at home requires endless lists, instructions for my mom, carpool arrangements, and should be considered an Olympic sport, gold-medal-worthy. Sometimes it felt like it wasn't even worth going, considering all the prep work it involved.

I actually counted the minutes until I was able to sit alone on an airplane, with a good book and a plastic cup filled with all the wine it would hold: paradise, a much-needed quiet respite. I was a tired mama in dire need of a break, and alone time with the husband I missed so much was just what I needed. Any fear that something might be going on with Dawson slowly subsided during the hectic few days before I left. But as soon as I took a breath and settled into my seat, my thoughts immediately went straight to him.

When I returned a few days later, I was anxious to see the kids. I was rested and ready to be a mom again. I put my bags down and immediately went into the playroom, where Dawson was quietly and intently sitting on the floor watching a movie.

"Dawsie! Mommy is back!" I cheerfully exclaimed.

His back was to me, and while he turned to the sound of my voice, his face was a complete blank, as if he had no idea who I was. The first thing that came to my mind was that maybe I was gone too long and he momentarily forgot about me. I could not imagine that being gone for only three days could make my baby forget about me. I picked him up to snuggle and suddenly had a chilling feeling that something was not right. What was it? Maybe he was just still not feeling well.

"Mom?" I asked, "has everything been okay with Dawson? Has he been acting like he might be getting sick again?"

"Not that I have noticed, sweetie, but I have been a little busy with those active girls of yours since the minute you left!" she said with a little laugh. "But he has been a little off, now that I think about it. Maybe he is getting more teeth."

A few days later we were back at the pediatrician's office because, sure enough, he did get sick again. We were now going on two months straight of antibiotics—antibiotics that just never seemed to relieve his ear infections or respiratory issues. The bowel issues continued as well, but I figured it was from all the medicine wreaking havoc on his GI tract. But he just wasn't himself, he wasn't Dawson. Something was wrong.

I told the doctor how he wasn't interested in his surroundings anymore. He was fixated on certain toys and would sit and spin the wheels on toy cars or anything that would spin. It was like he was locked in his own little world when he was doing those things, and nothing could distract him. He was completely entranced by The Wiggles, a colorful group of Australian men who sang catchy songs. He would flap his hands wildly while staring at the television, as if in a trance.

Then the tantrums started, in full force and over things that were not easily noticeable. He would scream in a state of almost panic if we took a left turn in the car, or when we would go into a store while in his stroller at the mall. I told all of this to the doctor; but by far, the most worrisome thing was that Dawson had lost the few words he had been saying.

"I'm sure everything is fine, Sarah," the doctor said casually. "I bet he's just the classic youngest boy with three older sisters that do ALL the talking for him."

As much as I wanted that to be true, I just was not buying it.

The doctor suggested that we have him evaluated by a specialist to see if we could come up with a reason for the sudden change in his personality. The appointment was made, but there was quite a long wait to get in, and it made me anxious to wait so long. I was ready to try whatever medication or treatment was needed to get our baby boy back to the way he was. It even crossed my mind that perhaps he had lost some hearing from all the ear infections, and I made a mental note to schedule a hearing test. It seemed like that would be an easy fix. I called my mom to fill her in on everything that was going on and told her how nervous I was about the upcoming appointment.

Then my mom said it. "Do you think he might have autism?"

I immediately, loudly and defensively said, "**NO WAY**!!" He was perfectly fine a month ago, other than being sick a lot. Kids don't just become autistic out of nowhere. But her comment haunted me and I couldn't shake it.

That evening, after all the kids were tucked in bed and Greg was at the ballpark, I looked up "Symptoms of Autism" on the computer. I stared at the screen for what seemed like an eternity as tears welled up in my eyes. This could not be true! Dawson had almost every single symptom listed.

August 28th, 2002, is a date etched in my brain for all eternity. What happened that day lives in my mind like a distant memory, but when I choose to go there, it's as if it just happened. Just the day before, we had celebrated Hayley's thirteenth birthday, in full Swindell fashion, by reserving the entire indoor pool at Bank One Ballpark. All her friends were there, it was huge and over the top. We didn't have the faintest idea that this day, full of laughter and celebration, would be the last for a long time to come. It would be our last day as a "normal" family.

I still vividly remember the smell in the doctor's waiting room, it was like the waiting room of an institution. We had never been to this doctor before, and her office did not look anything like a standard pediatrician's office. I distinctly remember flashing to a scene from *One Flew Over the Cuckoo's Nest*, and I quickly tried to shake it off. I told myself that it was just a very cold and sterile doctor's office. I knew instinctively that I hated it.

Parents and their children sat all around us. They all looked like they were trying not to think about the news that might be handed to them about their precious child. I imagine Greg and I had the very same look of fear on our faces.

"What do you think she is going to have him do?" I asked Greg, trying to break up our nervous silence.

"I have no idea. It's not like she can ask him questions or anything," he said with a shrug.

Dawson was sitting on the floor, staring intently at a speck of paper, as if it were a treasure. He would not take his eyes off it. Both of us knew what we would probably hear, but just below the surface, we were intently praying to be wrong. We prayed for a magic pill that would take him back to the Dawson he was just a few months earlier; we would wake up and it would just be a bad dream. I was desperately holding on to hope with every inch of my being, hope that we would walk out of that awful place smiling, relieved at how wrong we were.

I told myself that Dawson would look back at old videos and say, "WOW, what the heck was wrong with me back then?" We all would sit around and joke about how silly we were to be so scared that anything was ever wrong.

I was swiftly yanked from my hopeful thoughts as I heard his name called by the stone-faced nurse standing in the doorway. Dawson didn't even look up from his beloved tiny piece of paper—not responding to his name anymore was now the new normal. We scooped him up and followed the nurse to the child psychologist's office. It was a tiny playroom with deceptively vibrant, colorful blocks and brightly colored toys. Greg and I sat down on an uncomfortably small sofa, across from the small desk where the doctor sat. She looked over the notes that I assumed our pediatrician had sent over, as well as the paperwork I'd filled out in the waiting room. She asked us a few questions that I don't even remember answering. I just wanted the whole ordeal to be over as soon as possible.

What I do remember about the endless hour while Dawson was being tested, is that I could barely keep it together. His whole future hung on what that one doctor would say. I remember every task she tried to get Dawson to do, and each felt like a strike against him, over and over again. It broke my heart to see him struggle with the simplest requests. It broke my heart even more that he was being put through such scrutiny, it was an unnatural kind of observation.

I choked back tears as I silently cheered Dawson on to do the very best he could. I willed him to fool her into thinking nothing was seriously wrong and we didn't need her stupid opinion after all. When the test was over, she sat at her desk with her arms folded and started to speak. At that moment everything faded to black. My ears were ringing and I felt my throat swell as I tried to push back the sobs that were forming deep within my soul.

I remember thinking, *So this is what an out-of-body experience is.* I wanted to grab Dawson off the floor and run out of that office as fast as I could, but Greg had beat me to it. He picked up our son without saying a word and quickly walked out the door. I just sat there, my ears still ringing and silent tears streaming down my face, realizing that she had actually said what we so desperately did not want to hear, but already knew.

The doctor across the table spoke. "Your son has autism, and I believe it is a severe form. There are places for kids like him as he gets older," and "He will most likely never speak or go to a regular school and will probably need lifelong care." How the hell did she know all this about our eighteen-month-old son after only one hour with him? To hear someone say that Dawson had autism, to say it out loud and then continue on to tell me how severe it was, was a blow I was not prepared to receive. She handed me a single sheet of paper with all the therapies he needed and a bundle of pamphlets with information for newly diagnosed families.

Was this real? It felt like my son had just died, but there would be no funeral or memorial service to mourn the life we dreamed he would have. That dream was now, in a matter of one hour, gone forever. The doctor gently patted my back, told me she was sorry, wished me luck and said to call with any questions. Seriously? Any questions?

## Chapter 8

As I slowly walked through the parking lot to the car where Greg and Dawson were waiting, a movie of Dawson's short little life played on fast-forward in my head. I climbed into the passenger seat of our SUV, while the sobs I had stuffed down for over an hour suddenly came pouring out of me like dark, heavy rain.

CHAPTER 9

THE DRIVE HOME FROM THAT dreaded appointment seemed almost unreal. I silently watched the cars next to me, looking at the people inside. Those people looked so happy and content in their lives, smiling and laughing with the others in the car. Didn't they know my life and my son's life had just ended? How dare they continue to have a happy, normal life while ours was coming apart at the seams. I was suddenly jealous of them and knew that I would never be happy or smile, ever again.

My thoughts were racing. Greg was silent next to me with the most sullen look on his face that I had ever seen. We said nothing as we pulled into the McDonald's drive-thru to get Dawson his beloved french fries.

I immediately thought of Karie, my dear friend who I'd become extremely close to, whose husband worked for the Diamondbacks front offices. Her daughter, who was just a little older than Dawson, was blind with cerebral palsy, and Karie was dealing with her own devastating situation. I had confided in her about my fears that something was wrong in the few months leading up to Dawson's diagnosis, and we often leaned on each other when it came to our precious, imperfect babies. I felt comfort that I was not alone whenever we had our long talks, and I needed to hear her voice immediately.

My hands shook uncontrollably as I dug my cell phone out of my purse and called. When Kari answered, I could not even get the words out of my mouth as my throat swelled up, trying again not to cry. She knew about the appointment and understood exactly what I was trying to say. As a good friend would, she listened quietly. Once I could start talking she just kept saying "I'm sorry," which is all I wanted to hear. I didn't want a pep talk, or to be told all will be okay. I wanted someone to feel sorry for me, not try to pretend it wasn't as bad as it really was, and she knew that.

I told Greg to pull over at a Barnes & Noble on our way home. I needed more information about autism immediately and wanted to buy every single book I could get my hands on. I walked into the store with swollen eyes and had no idea where to start. Was it where the medical books were? The Psychology section, or the section on Child Development? I had no idea, and my head felt like a lead weight from all that had happened in the last two hours. I walked to the information desk in the middle of the store.

I barely got one word out before the tears started falling again. I am sure the girl at the counter must have thought something was seriously wrong with me, and she was right. I was a mom who felt as if her son had just died, and I needed information fast on how to deal with it.

Then I heard an angelic voice behind me: "I can help you find books on autism. My son is autistic." I literally fell into this poor innocent lady's arms.

"I don't know you at all, but I do know exactly how you feel," she said. Her name was Gayle. I don't remember everything she said, but I knew that God had placed this very lady, in this very store, at this very moment to help me. Her son Kyle was nineteen and profoundly autistic.

## Chapter 9

"Kyle has changed me for the better in countless ways," she continued, "and the pain you are feeling now will not be forever, but it won't always be easy."

Gayle gave me her number that day, and we spoke several times in the weeks that followed. Dawson is now the same age as Kyle was when I met Gayle, and she was 100 percent right about everything we talked about during our long conversations. Her soft, kind voice helped me work through so many hard questions. She was always honest, but also very careful to not scare me with each and every difficult detail. Sometimes she would talk, but mostly she simply listened, which was exactly what I needed during those dark early days. I left the bookstore that day not only with a pile of books, but with a welcome sense of calmness, thanks to Gayle. She was the first of many *autism angels* who would come into my life.

For the entire week that followed, Greg and I both had horrible nightmares. Sometimes we would cry and sometimes would just silently hold each other without saying a word. Trying to keep it together in front of our girls was almost impossible. Hayley was old enough to understand how serious the diagnosis was for Dawson, and she was busy doing her own research on autism. For Brenna and Sophia, they may not have entirely understood what autism was, but they knew they had lost their baby brother in a way, and that life was going to be very different.

The girls sensed that Mom and Dad needed some time to regroup and mourn what had happened to Dawson. They were extra patient and on their best behavior around the house, instinctively giving us space. As young as they were, I think they knew their lives as Dawson's sisters had changed and were likely a little scared.

As much as I tried to keep it together, I cried a lot, and I mean a lot. My eyes were constantly swollen, and I would burst into tears for no reason—just giving him a bath, changing his diaper, or putting him to bed. Everything in our lives was now so incredibly different, like we were sucked out of our old life and dropped head first into a new one, landing with a giant thud.

I remember how quiet Greg was. He has always been a man of few words, but he was absolutely struggling in his own silence. It worried me how much he wasn't talking about it. Not only was his world at home falling apart, he was struggling professionally on the mound. For something that used to be so important to me, baseball was now the last thing I cared about. I now had more important work to tend to at home with only one thing on my mind—CURE DAWSON.

After a few weeks of crying and sleepless nights, it was time to dust ourselves off, wipe away the tears and get to work. "Applied Behavior Analysis," also known as ABA if you're into acronyms, quickly became front and center in our world. It was one of the things written on that piece of paper the doctor gave me, and it was the first one I researched. To me, it sounded like a sterile set of words. I imagined kids in little cages with doctors wearing white lab coats holding clipboards jotting down observations of that child and how they were behaving. I wasn't that far off in my guess.

I have a love/hate relationship with ABA. The protocol in 2002 was that the newly diagnosed child would need forty hours of therapy a week to have a fighting chance at a possible recovery, and the word "cure" was thrown around a lot. At eighteen months old, Dawson was considered extremely young to be diagnosed and a prime candidate for ABA to work its apparent magic. I wanted to cure Dawson more than anything else in the world.

It was, and still is, no easy task navigating the autism world. There was so much information available, but no clear-cut way to treat it, or one way to go about it. It felt like walking blindly into a long, dark hallway with hundreds of doors; only one had the answer to curing autism, and we had to find the right one blindfolded.

## Chapter 9

Before we started the intense process of **ABA**, Dawson's pediatrician thought it would be a good idea to rule out anything and everything else that could possibly mimic autism or cause symptoms that sometimes appear in autistic children. I had never even considered that maybe it wasn't autism, or that it could be something else, something fixable! Maybe that lady was wrong, and I would be able to march back into her office in a few months to tell her just how terribly wrong she was.

It took about a month and numerous appointments with every kind of doctor there was. We held out hope that maybe he had become deaf from all the ear infections, or maybe allergic to certain foods. We started a gluten-free, dairy-free diet because we read about how just eliminating those two things could cure autism.

*How easy would that be!* I thought. We checked for seizures, had **MRI**s and **CT** scans. I even prayed they would find a brain tumor. At least with a tumor, it could be removed, and then we'd have a treatment plan to work with. I would have accepted just about anything in place of a lifelong neurobiological disorder with no cure and no treatment plan to follow.

As crazy as it sounds, Greg and I started doing a shot of any type of alcohol we had at home before we left the house for each doctor appointment. Even as I write this, it sounds a little strange, but it seemed to calm our nerves quite nicely. We left each appointment with either more bad news, a shoulder shrug, or a head scratch from the doctor who had no clue what to say about what to do next. That tiny shot got us through each disappointing appointment and the utter frustration that doctors did not know anything about his mysterious disorder.

Dawson wasn't deaf, he did not have a brain tumor, and the new diet wasn't curing anything. It was autism, and there was no way around it. It was time to accept it and hit the ground running with this **ABA** thing that I now was convinced was going to save him. We would be *that* success story. I knew that in a short time we would be sharing our amazing journey to a successful recovery with the world. We would be on every talk show and news channel in the country, talking about how Applied Behavioral Analysis saved our child and how it could save yours too. That is exactly what my overly excited brain was thinking.

We hired our first **ABA** therapist, Allen, just as Dawson turned nineteen months old. We turned one of the rooms in our house into a full-fledged therapy classroom, exactly as we were told to do. It was complete with a small table, two chairs, specific toys, and positive reinforcements to keep his tantrums under control. Allen was a kind and gentle young man who had a younger autistic brother and extensive training in **ABA**. He was eager to start working with Dawson and was confident that because Dawson was so young, he had a good chance of getting better. Dawson was the youngest child Allen had ever worked with, and I wasn't sure if that was good or bad. I still had the word *"cured"* tucked neatly in my head, but tried to not get ahead of myself and take each day one at a time with as much patience as I could muster.

Greg and I were not anywhere near prepared for what this type of therapy would be like for our son. The screaming and crying we heard from behind the closed doors was almost more than we could bear. Dawson was only nineteen months old, and it sounded like he was being tortured by a total stranger in our own home. We were allowing it to happen, we were actually paying someone to torture our son.

Greg and I would hold each other, and I would remind myself that it was the right thing.

"This is fucking bullshit," Greg would angrily say as we sat nearby. "There is no way this can be good for him."

But we were told over and over by Allen to please be patient, that in the end it would be worth all the suffering. But more than once, the screams and sheer terror we listened to on the other side of that door made us question what we were doing. It made me question what kind of mother would allow this to happen to her own child. Was I actually helping him, or hurting him?

It would go on for two or three hours at a time, at least six days a week, and sometimes two different sessions of three hours in one day. It took everything we had not to burst into that room and demand it all stop. Greg actually did that a few times when he just couldn't take it anymore, and I didn't stop him. There is no question Allen cared deeply for Dawson and did his very best to help him. It was unexplored territory for all of us, and we all had the same goal for him, which was to reverse the autism, no matter what it took.

During this time, I was so focused on Dawson I did not see how much Greg was struggling in his own mind. I was no longer the wife he once had who was filled with smiles and laughter; the wife who was his biggest cheerleader at the ballpark and a loving, involved mother at home. I had changed. Autism had changed me. Autism had stolen my son and was now in the process of stealing my marriage.

CHAPTER 10

THE FIRST YEAR OF DAWSON's diagnosis, during 2002 and 2003, was a blur. I honestly do not remember much about it, other than being consumed by the pressure to get in forty hours a week of therapy for him, doctor visits, and going to every autism conference I could get to. Sadly, I don't remember much about what my daughters were up to in their personal lives. I do remember attending dance recitals, managing playdates and birthday parties for them, but never feeling that I was totally in the moment with any of it.

I knew Hayley was starting to get very interested in boys, and I was trying to keep an eye on that situation the best I could. I think I pretended to be interested in everything going on around me, but if it wasn't about autism, I sincerely wasn't. All I cared about was figuring out what happened to my little boy. I was obsessed, to say the least. Extremely tired and obsessed were the only words to describe myself during that time.

On top of all the moving parts going on in our house, Greg was still struggling with the Diamondbacks and just wasn't looking like his old self on the field. The team made it to the first round of the playoffs in 2002, but was quickly eliminated from advancing any further; it seemed that the magic had run its course. Greg's hip was really starting to bother him from years of wear and tear, and his numbers were starting to show it. At only thirty-seven years old, he had been playing for almost seventeen years, and we silently knew the end had to be coming soon but never really discussed it. I didn't want to bring up anything that might hurt his already-suffering ego and just tried to stay as positive as possible.

I don't know if Dawson's situation played a direct role in the last year of Greg's baseball career, but it certainly didn't help his game. Greg was not always good about sharing his personal thoughts and feelings, but I do know that his only son's future being as fragile as it was, was terribly painful for him to accept. He was heartbroken, and I knew that. I also knew he constantly worried about me and how I was handling everything while he was on road trips. Even with all the help I had, it was incredibly emotionally and physically draining at times. I was continuously sleep deprived because Dawson was up so much at night, screaming like he was in some sort of pain. I can't imagine that it did not directly impact Greg's ability to focus on the game, when I could hardly focus on anything other than keeping my head above water.

Another angel in our lives at that time was Greg's older sister, Chrystie. Shortly after Dawson's diagnosis, she selflessly left her life in Texas and moved to Arizona to live with us. Chrystie was the kind of girl that you instantly wanted in your life. Like Greg, she was very quiet and was more of an observer than a talker. She had a warmth about her that was instantly calming, and she always had words of encouragement after a rough day. She loved our kids as if they were her own and was on a mission to help Dawson any way she could.

Chrystie even took classes on **ABA** and learned strategies and techniques so she could work with Dawson when the therapist wasn't there. We were literally bombarding Dawson with therapy to try and reverse the damage that had been done to his brain. Chrystie gave us emotional support as well. She would often sit and cry with us on days we felt defeated, or be a shining light with her infectious laugh when Dawson would make a tiny breakthrough. We also still had Maria helping us out and could never have made it without her love, kindness and heartfelt support. Dawson was like Maria's own son. She had been there since the day he was born. I knew she worried just as much as we did.

My parents would fly in for a few days here and there so I could meet up with Greg on the road for a little respite, or just for moral support when things got really tough at home. I wanted to do my very best to keep things as normal as possible and make sure my marriage was taken care of just as much as my children were. Those little trips helped so much. Dawson's support team saved me in so many ways, I can't imagine how I would have gotten through those early years without them by my side.

The girls rallied around him, doing all they could to help their beloved, lost baby brother. Brenna, especially, would follow Dawson around the house, trying to engage with him any way she could. Even though she was only eight years old at the time, it was like she knew we had to get him back into our world. Brenna would quietly sit and observe the therapy sessions as if she was trying to learn the techniques herself. We would catch her later trying to work with Dawson on her own. We all had no idea what we were doing, but we always had a nagging feeling that *time was of the essence*.

When you have a baby, it's like you're setting out on the ultimate road trip with no map or GPS to guide you. When we started Dawson's road trip, we got a nail in the tire before we even left our neighborhood. Our journey continued to be unpredictable and scary at times, and I was constantly looking for new ideas about what to try next. I attended an autism conference that year, where I met Dr. Andrew Wakefield. He was a British gastroenterologist, forced to leave his practice in England after he published a case series in *The Lancet* about the possible correlation between the MMR vaccine and autism in 1998.

I realize this is a very touchy and controversial subject, but I refuse to be silenced by fear of what people may say or think about what we believed happened, what I believed happened to our son. There is no denying that Dawson quickly regressed within days, if not *the* day he received his routine vaccines. Prior to receiving his last round of shots, Dawson had several words in his vocabulary, he was engaged with his surroundings, and had imitation skills. He smiled, laughed and had perfect eye contact. In less than one week, all of it simply vanished. When I look back at all of his records, I see a pattern. After each shot he got sicker and sicker with ear infections and loose stools, but his personality was still there. I was just doing what the doctors were telling me do, just like I had done with all three girls. But the feeling that I was the one who pulled the trigger that ended Dawson's life, so to speak, has never gone away. He was never the same again after that last round of shots. His life was forever changed.

I believe with all my heart that all the antibiotics he was on were destroying his gut and his immune system. When live viruses are injected into a compromised immune system, there is no way that can be good. I am not a doctor or a scientist by any means, but I have spent the last seventeen years of my life researching what may have happened to Dawson. Let me be clear, I am not against childhood vaccines and am a believer in the good that Western medicine can provide to very sick people; my son included. However, I do believe a safer protocol should be used, as this is not a one-size-fits-all situation. The bottom line is, if it is just as easy for the "experts" to suggest that pesticides, among other environmental issues, may cause autism, why can't a syringe filled with live viruses and other toxic ingredients be a possibility as well? It is no different than thinking stress can cause cancer.

My twenty-nine-year-old daughter received nine shots before the age of two. Now babies are required to receive over thirty-five different vaccines before the same age. Who did the research on the long-term safety of so many shots in that little time? I realize not all babies will react to routine vaccines, just as not every smoker will get lung cancer, but the possibility for lung cancer goes up the more you smoke. I'm a very reasonable person and have always been open to any other ideas as to what happened to my son. I was going to do anything in my power, as any mother would, to turn over every stone out there in order to help him. His obvious adverse reaction to that round of vaccines has haunted me every day for years. It's the only thing that ever made any sense, and I believed it more than ever after I attended one particular conference and met Dr. Andrew Wakefield.

As I sat and listened to Dr. Wakefield's presentation for the first time, tears rolled down my face as he described his research and findings. He spoke about some of the mothers' stories and what happened to their children. To my horror, their stories were almost identical to mine. Most of them started with numerous ear infections and prolonged antibiotic use, followed by regression and bowel issues shortly after a routine vaccination. I immediately thought about that day in the driveway as my neighbor talked about delaying her son's vaccines because she was concerned about the autism connection. Why didn't I listen? I could have saved Dawson, but instead I felt like I had murdered him.

I fought so hard to control the flood of emotions and tears as I continued to listen to Dr. Wakefield. I lost that battle. I looked around the room at the hundreds of other parents, mostly mothers, and noticed they looked just like me—scared, heartbroken and with tears in their eyes. I started to look at all those women as if they would be my new family, a club I wanted nothing to do with, but would join whether I liked it or not. I had a sudden urge to spring up out of my seat and hug each and every one of them. I wanted to tell them how sorry I was about what they were going through, because I understood and felt the very same way they did. A sudden feeling of extreme closeness to this group of complete strangers was followed by a new sense of calm. I was not alone in this fight.

It never *really* hit me until that day at the conference, that this is what might have happened to Dawson. Every word Dr. Wakefield spoke felt as if he was describing my own personal story. Everything he said made sense to me, and for the first time that year, I felt like we finally had something to navigate by. If we could figure out the cause, maybe there would be a specific treatment plan that would actually work! Maybe Dawson was in so much physical pain from the inflammation in his belly that his brain was just not working properly. *Cure the pain, cure the brain,* I thought.

During this time, Dawson was having bowel movements at least ten times a day. I wouldn't even call them bowel movements, they were more like a frothy, foamy mess of easily recognizable undigested food. While no poop is pretty, his was a whole other kind of animal with a smell that had no proper descriptive word to go with it. Whatever it was, it wasn't right, and we had to find a way to get some much-needed relief for him. I had no doubt in my mind that the doctor standing at that podium was the answer.

After Dr. Wakefield finished speaking, I, along with every other distraught mother in the room, fought my way up to him with the hope of talking to him personally. It felt like it was Black Friday and we were all clawing our way to the front of the store, about to claim our deal of a lifetime. Only in this case, the deal was saving our child. I finally reached him, and with pleading, desperate eyes, begged him for help. I used the "I'm married to a professional baseball player" card. I would do anything I could to grab his attention. By this point in the game, I would have done just about anything to help Dawson. I got his contact information and felt like I had just won the lottery. This was the first glimmer of anything even close to resembling hope.

A few months later, the Diamondbacks released Greg. Baseball had finally come to an end after seventeen unforgettable years. He could have kept going in the minor leagues with the hopes of being called up again, but between his bad hip and the stress of autism, he decided it was finally a good time to retire. This may sound like a great thing to most people, because who wouldn't want to retire at thirty-eight years old with plenty of money in the bank? Ask any baseball player, retired or not, how much they love what they do, and they will tell you they would never retire if that was an option. Any professional athlete, no matter what the sport, would probably say the same thing.

Losing the one thing that made Greg who he was for so long felt like another death. He lost a big part of his identity, his purpose, and the special friendships with the teammates he saw every day for eight months in a row for seventeen years. He went from being a celebrity to being just a regular guy with nothing to do anymore, and no one really seemed to care. I know that still doesn't seem too terrible, but it was for him. I believe the combination of being let go by the team he loved, combined with the constant stress of what was happening to his son, was too much for him. He was a guy who didn't express feelings about stuff like that; he held it all in. On the other hand, I was personally thrilled to have another set of hands to help with all that was going on at home, and I was glad the traveling days were over. Not only did I miss Greg so much when he was gone, now I didn't have to do it alone anymore.

Dawson continued to struggle through all of his therapies. We were all getting beat down by Dawson's lack of progress and the constant revolving door of people in our home. Greg seemed lost to me, not really knowing what to do with himself, now that he wasn't heading to the ballpark anymore. I was plenty busy managing the kids and Dawson's rigorous schedule with caregivers while trying to keep the constant tantrums at bay. Greg was very helpful and would do anything I needed, but he just was not himself, not at all. Maybe we all were not ourselves.

A few months into his retirement, I started to feel a subtle shift in our marriage. I knew the stats on all the failed marriages surrounding autism, along with the stats on being married to a retired professional athlete. I was never going to let that happen to us. I truly believed our marriage was stronger than most. I know many couples go through an adjustment period after a spouse retires, from any profession, but this seemed different. Something was happening between us that I just couldn't quite put my finger on. I felt like something bad was simmering, just waiting to boil over.

# CHAPTER 11

We MOVED HOUSES AT LEAST three times from 2003 to 2004. One would think that moving with four children, not to mention one with very special needs, would not be considered a fun thing or a good idea. The kids didn't seem to mind much because they never had to change schools, as each house we moved to was in the same school district. Greg didn't mind as long as he didn't have to help with the process, and my mom enjoyed it, so I had no problem with it. Since we always moved close to the last house, it would take about a week to shuttle our small items over to the new house. So by the time the furniture was set to be moved, everything was already there, without any boxes to unpack. I had developed a systematic method to my madness.

Clearly, it was not always a good financial decision, after broker fees, moving expenses, etc. But I didn't care, I loved it, and I loved the physical labor it required. It was a huge rush for me, and I had a tremendous amount of satisfaction when it was over. Most of all, it took my mind off everything bad that was going on.

Early in 2004, we decided to move to Austin, Texas. Greg was offered the volunteer coach position for the Texas State baseball team where his best friend was the head coach. Greg didn't finish college at

The University of Texas at Austin because he was drafted as a first-round pick his junior year. The plan was for him to try and finish college so he could eventually become a paid coach. Not long after coaching at Texas State, he became the volunteer coach for the Texas Longhorns. He was thrilled to be back with the team that changed the path of his life. Unfortunately, we were entering full-blown marriage crisis by this point, and Dawson was at his very worst, which did not help the situation.

Greg and I never really fought, but there was an undeniable tension between us. I would get easily annoyed if Greg sat around watching T V all day, and I felt I was doing everything, from taking care of the kids to managing the house. Even though I did all those same things when Greg was playing ball, now we had a child with special needs, and home life was very different than it used to be.

He would do anything if I asked, but I didn't want to *ask*. Like most women, I wanted him to read my mind and just DO it without me asking. Obviously not a reasonable thing to expect from anyone. There came a point when we stopped having fun together and rarely talked about anything other than the kids. We even stopped talking about what we needed to do next for Dawson. Most of the time, I felt like I was the only one doing the talking and making decisions, while he quietly listened without much feedback.

At first I thought the change of scenery from Arizona to Texas would be good for both of us, that it would give Greg a chance to get back to the baseball world he missed so much. But all it really did was make me feel like I was raising our children by myself all over again.

Dawson was still hardly sleeping, and along with being in constant pain, this led to consistent tantrums. He was covered in bruises from beating his own body against anything he could find to ease his pain. Thankfully, I had stayed in touch with Dr. Wakefield and was beyond thrilled to learn that he and his family were moving to Austin to open an autism resource center. Hope was finally on the way.

## Chapter 11

One afternoon Greg came into the kitchen and asked, "What do you think about me coming out of retirement and giving it another shot?"

The way his face lit up just talking about it was proof enough of how much he wanted to do it. I immediately told him I was on board. He quickly got on the phone with his agent and was soon invited to Kansas City's spring training camp. He was thirty-nine years old, but felt confident he had what it took to make the team. To make it even more exciting, we found out our favorite country singer, Garth Brooks, was going to be there for the entire spring training. It was a dream of Garth's to play along with a major league team, and a dream of Greg's to hang out with his idol.

On Valentine's Day 2004, Greg left for spring training like he always had, with a sweet card and a long, tearful goodbye. I was hopeful that this would bring a little zip back in our marriage and would return Greg back to his old self again. There was no way I could have joined him for spring training, the kids were in school, and I was not about to travel with Dawson. I was still traumatized by the last time I flew with him. That two-hour flight was filled with endless tantrums, and by the time we touched down, I was literally covered in poop from his diaper that had leaked. Nope, never again. It was going to be a long six weeks, but I had a sense that this was going to be the best thing for us, and most of all for Greg.

It was one of the best spring trainings Greg ever had. Even more incredible, Greg and Garth became buddies. We were later invited to spend a weekend in Oklahoma with Garth and Trisha Yearwood, on their houseboat, on their private lake, on their property. Having Garth Brooks pick us up from the airport and Trisha Yearwood cook us breakfast is definitely on our Top 5 List of best moments ever.

We were confident that Greg would make the final roster that spring, and we both felt a renewed sense of excitement after a very difficult two years. We desperately needed a bright spot, and I desperately wanted my happy husband back, doing what he loved and had missed so much.

"I was cut, babe," Greg told me on the phone.

On the last day of spring training Greg was told he didn't make the team. He was devastated; we both were in shock. He could not have proved himself any more than he did during that spring, but it just wasn't enough. He would once again have to endure the emotions of losing his career. We were all too soon back to the reality. Now we needed to stay focused on our girls, on Dawson, AND on us.

One night about a month later, Dawson was thrashing around so badly we were afraid he might really hurt himself. He had lost a great deal of weight and looked nothing like a healthy three-year-old should look. No doctor could explain his uncontrollable bowel issues, they would just say it was probably the stress of the autism. By this point, I was convinced, more than ever, that it was all vaccine-related. I researched everything I could get my hands on, and Dr. Wakefield's theory was the only thing that continued to make any sense to me.

On this particular night, we had had enough of watching Dawson's miserable and painful life continue with no answers. It was late when I frantically called Dr. Wakefield to see if he was willing to come over to see what was going on. Thankfully, he arrived at our house a short time later, and we walked him upstairs to Dawson's room. He watched with a concerned look as Dawson twisted and contorted on the floor, screaming as if he was being ravaged by a pack of lions.

Dr. Wakefield quickly told us that we needed to get him on a plane as soon as we could, to get him to a gastroenterologist in New York. This doctor had been helping children with autism and bowel issues just like Dawson. It was soon confirmed that Dawson had ulcerative colitis, and he was put on medications and a very restrictive diet. Thankfully, the pain that Dawson had been living with for two years got markedly better, but would continue to be an issue for him to this day.

# Chapter 11

Even though he seemed to feel a little better, my dream of curing Dawson was slowly fading away. He was not making the progress I had read about other children making, and he still could not speak at all, despite all the speech therapy we were doing. His speech therapist eventually diagnosed him with apraxia and kindly told us to be prepared that he may never speak. Everything that doctor told us a few years earlier was slowly and painfully becoming a reality. It made me feel so defeated to think that we may never be the success story I had once dreamed of.

I was feeling nothing like my old self and was cranky and irritable at home. I felt like I was always snapping at the girls, and I am sure I was not the nicest wife, either. While I knew it was not true deep in my heart, it seemed like Greg only cared about Longhorn baseball and was voluntarily gone all the time. I was starting to resent the fact that he was gone while there was so much to deal with at home. Looking back, I realize that he probably wanted to run away from our situation as much as I did; like so many other moms do, I tried to keep it all together despite everything.

A month or so after moving to Austin, I met Stacy while I was on a walk with Dawson. At the time, we were living in a cramped apartment while our house was being built, so I tried to get out as often as possible. Dawson loved going for walks in his stroller; this seemed to be the only time he was actually still. I loved those walks as well and took advantage of them as often as I could. I had a plastic cup filled with wine in the cup holder of the stroller and walked the apartment parking lot in circles like a track, killing time before dinner. As I walked, a pretty girl with long brown hair, slender build and a bag full of groceries came up to us.

"When did you guys move in?" she asked with a friendly smile.

"We bought a house in Silver Oaks, and it's still in the building process. We just moved here from Arizona, and I'm feeling a little stir-crazy with four kids in a small apartment!" I responded, happy to be talking to a grown-up.

I instantly liked her and knew I had made my first Austin friend. She soon introduced me to her circle, and in no time, our little group was inseparable. We were the proverbial Ladies Who Lunch, and we pretty much did everything together. It became a bond that felt more like a sisterhood than friendship, and there was rarely a day that went by when we didn't see each other. We were in our prime, financially secure and had kids around the same age. Greg and I seemed to be communicating much better, and I felt like we were a team again. Things were finally starting to look up.

Hayley, Brenna and Sophia were incredibly helpful, as always. They were understanding about all the attention Dawson needed and how that impacted us as a family. We rarely let them have sleepovers once we moved into our house. We never knew if Dawson would be up all night; and frankly, I just didn't want to deal with any more children in the house. Hayley was having a bit of a hard time, she missed Arizona tremendously. I completely understood her feelings. I remembered feeling the same thing, being in the same position, at the same age.

So what did we do? In 2006, we moved back to Arizona, just one year after we left. We decided that the services in Arizona were much better for Dawson. At first, Hayley was relieved at the idea of going back. But by the time we sold our home and it came time to leave, Hayley had fallen in love with Austin. She also had a new boyfriend which may have played a part, but it was too late to turn back, and we set off for the desert once again.

That year is extremely fuzzy. I just remember always feeling tired, out of sorts and never quite settled like I'd hoped I would. It may have been because we never seemed to really *be* settled, but to me, it was more than that. I remember days of profound sadness that would come upon me, triggered when driving by a Little League field, seeing little boys running and laughing, knowing that would never be my son; or after seeing a happy family at a restaurant without a care in the world. Going out to dinner was nearly impossible with Dawson. I found myself dwelling on the future and what that was, or was *not*, going to look like for us.

Once again, Greg and I were drifting farther and farther apart. We were back to not communicating, and quite simply, I felt totally alone in a home full of people. I wrote in my journal almost every night. I wish I still had that journal, because now everything is so unclear to me as to what exactly was going on during that time. I do distinctly remember crying a lot more than I should have been. I know that I am a pretty good crier anyway, but this felt different. Maybe it was real depression, who knows. I don't know why I never talked to a professional about it, but I should have; it might have changed everything.

So what did I do to make myself feel better? I found us a new house, because that clearly kept solving all my problems! Unfortunately, shortly after moving into that house, Greg and I separated.

CHAPTER 12

THAT FIRST SEPARATION DIDN'T LAST very long and maybe doesn't even count as a real separation. I call it that because a bag was packed and Greg left for a few days. That bag would lovingly become known as the *bye-bye bag* since it was the one he always used when he would leave.

Sadly, we would end up separating a few more times during the next few years, and I can't even really remember why. There were never loud arguments or name-calling. It would just happen, and I honestly can't recall how it was decided that it would be better if Greg just left.

Looking back, there is no way the kids were not affected, but I don't even remember them saying anything or asking any questions. Each separation would last longer and longer, but would never last more than a couple of months. The crazy part was, we would still get together during the separations and have sex, quite regularly.

I would anxiously wait for the door chime to sound very late at night, alerting me that Greg was there. I would hear him pad down the hallway to our bedroom as my heart pounded with anticipation, and he would quietly crawl into bed with me. It just seemed like the natural and normal thing to do. It was an example of the undeniable chemistry we always had, even during the worst of times.

Right before that first mini separation, Greg was definitely going through something that he wasn't sharing with me. He would sit in his small TV room for most of the day. I remember feeling as if he just didn't want to be around any of us. I would peek in the room and he just would be entranced with the TV or his computer, content that we were all going about our lives without him. He just looked sad all the time.

For Dawson's fifth birthday, I planned a small birthday party in our neighborhood. Just a few parents and their kids came to hang out in our front yard. Greg never even came outside, not for any of it. I was already in a funk because Dawson had no clue it was his birthday. He had no desire to open gifts and couldn't even grasp the concept of blowing out candles. That day was just another reminder of all the milestones he was missing and how little progress we had made, despite all that we were doing. It hurt more than I could ever express at the time, to love your child so much and watch him struggle with the smallest of things—especially things that should bring joy to his life and never did. I needed Greg to share this hurt with me. Once again, I felt alone in my world of sadness and grief.

As I painted on my usually sunny smile, chatted with neighbors and watched the kids play the little games I had arranged, Dawson sat by himself, mesmerized by the repetitive action of throwing small rocks at the house over and over again. It wasn't until he had a tantrum that I went inside, and with a tone I am sure was not remotely nice, I asked Greg to come outside to help me, and he did. But I distinctly remember looking at the man I loved so much and for so long, thinking something's wrong; he doesn't look right. It's like he wanted to be anywhere other than with his family. As I think back to that day, was I thinking the same thing? The only difference was that I could fake it a little better than he could. Now I realize we were both officially dealing with some form of depression.

That year back in Arizona was a rough one. Being back in the place where everything had been so magical did not help one bit, it actually made things worse. We were not in baseball anymore, so we didn't have the friendships that were so readily available every night or on weekends at the ballpark. Much of the 2001 World Series team had all either retired or were playing on other teams in other states. I was lonely for some girl-time and missed my Austin friends tremendously. I leaned on Dawson's therapists who continued to work with him six days a week. Sometimes they were the only adult conversation I would have. I wonder now if they noticed all that was going on in our house or felt the tension brewing. I grew to love those kind young ladies and always looked forward to seeing their happy, carefree faces at my front door.

I looked forward to the times when they would come over to work with Dawson, as it meant I could step away for just a moment to have some free time. I loved when the session would end and we would sit to discuss Dawson's progress, always celebrating with a glass of wine after any tiny breakthrough. These girls were not only a gift to Dawson, but a gift to me in so many ways. Maria was back with us as well and still a huge part of our family. She literally kept our lives in order. The house always looked as if the perfect family lived inside, even if in reality it was a complete disaster. All the kids loved her, and I know she helped give our lives the much-needed stability we were starving for. I have never met a finer person, happily willing give so much of herself to our family.

This is where I need to admit that my own destructive and careless behavior began to surface. I felt lonely, was sad about my marriage being a mess, had an autistic child and three young girls who needed my attention. However! There is no excuse for how I started behaving. I started seeking attention from someone else. I desperately wanted something to take away all the junk that was floating around in my head. I was reverting back to my old high school self: When things got rough, surely the attention of a man could fix it. Not a mani/pedi, a shopping spree, a long walk, or a glass of wine could fix my troubled head. But a man telling me I was beautiful and amazing could. One day out of the blue I contacted Kyle, knowing I would hear what I needed, like an addict needing just one little hit.

"SAARRRAHHHH!" he excitedly shouted on the phone when I called him. "How did you know I was just thinking about you?"

Kyle and I were very close in high school, and he was my first real crush when I moved to Farmington. We became best friends in high school, and I always thought if I hadn't met Greg, we would have ended up together. He was good-looking, with a magnetic energy that made you just want to be around him, and a smile that lit up a room. We had stayed in touch here and there since high school, but it had been years since we had talked.

After a few long conversations on the phone with Kyle, I felt alive again. Kyle understood me and would listen when I talked about my thoughts and fears. I liked that we talked about what was going on in his life too. He would tell me how amazing I was and would make me laugh with all his long, animated stories.

I told myself that I was simply enjoying stimulating conversation with an old friend, and nothing was wrong with it. It also made me realize just how much Greg and I were not communicating after talking with Kyle, and I missed that. I wanted things to get back to how they were so badly. It was wrong to feel so happy talking to another man, and I knew it. But at that moment, Kyle was filling a void, and it felt good.

There was a very clear moment when I realized that Greg and I were in big trouble. Greg had just flown in to Phoenix from Austin from his volunteer coaching job with UT. I was completely exhausted physically and mentally, so I decided to take a hot bath after the kids went to bed. A few days earlier, Dawson had suffered what we thought was some kind of a stroke or maybe a seizure, we still don't even know; but whatever it was, it was a giant step backward, and I was terrified of what was happening. I felt all alone in my fears, and as I sat in the bathtub I started to cry. I was scared that so many things in my life were spiraling out of control. Greg walked into the bathroom and cooly patted my shoulder.

"Everything will be okay." Then he just continued getting ready for bed, without another word, as if nothing was wrong with me at all. He didn't even ask me why I was crying. I remember feeling a sudden rage that my husband didn't care enough about me to even talk to me or comfort me. It was a defining moment when I might have checked out of my marriage.

I was spending time looking for others to make me happy, when I should have been spending time figuring out why I needed that so much. At that point, we had drifted so far apart without realizing what was happening. Our marriage was like the *Titanic*, it was sinking from all the holes that had been bashed through it without clear warning. I think we were both doing what we needed to in order to survive. I don't know if Greg was chatting with girls from his past or doing anything that he shouldn't be doing, and to be honest, I have never asked him. Maybe that question doesn't need to be asked, and I don't think it would have mattered if he was.

I look back at my behavior and hate that part of me. I hate that I didn't fight harder to fix what was broken in my marriage. Instead, I put Band-Aids on something that was so precious and valuable to me, something I thought would last forever. We both got lazy, and instead of clinging to each other when things got rough, we pushed each other away without recognizing it.

Everyone's idea of an affair may differ, but I was no doubt having an emotional one. I felt so out of sorts all the time and was searching for anything to take my mind off whatever it was that I was going through. Was it my marriage troubles or the stress of having an autistic child? Looking back, it had to have been both of those worlds colliding.

I was so frightened by autism, I felt the window was closing on Dawson ever having the possibility of a recovery. He wasn't progressing like I had hoped, he was actually getting worse despite all our hard work. The whole thing had become overwhelming and demoralizing. I had no idea what to do next. I felt a paralyzing sense of hopelessness, and the pressure I put on myself to act like I was fine and had everything under control was speeding toward the boiling point.

As I sit and write this, it hurts my heart. I am filled with sadness that we let those painful events blur our strength and commitment to each other and how it turned me into a person I hated. I think we both became spoiled by the magical fairy-tale life of fame, fortune and a love for each other that seemed unbreakable. I wish my older self could have wrapped my arms around my younger self back then and said, "Sarah, **YES** this sucks ass big time, but you both need to get your shit together and fight for your family. This is so much bigger than your own feelings right now, and you will need each other more than you'll ever know down the road. Go on a nice date together, get a bottle of wine, talk about your feelings. **MOVE FORWARD** for Christ's sake!"

In 2007, it was time for another Swindell move—just because things were so boring in our lives. Seriously though, we did decide to pack up the family once again and head back to Austin for the second time. After years of reflecting on the reasons why we lived in an obscene number of different homes, my only conclusion is that not only did I enjoy the process, but it was an escape. I would get lost in the intense process of moving and forget about the bigger issues, plain and simple.

If I had it to do all over again, I would have just stayed put, especially for the kids. I am certain they were never able to feel completely settled throughout their childhood. Maybe they were so young they never learned what settled felt like. It makes me sad knowing they are never able to use the words "childhood home" and were never able to form strong friendships with neighborhood kids. I have seen the benefit that normalcy can bring to a child's life through both of my brothers' families. I am hopeful my daughters will be able to provide that for their own children someday, as I should have for them.

We thought this move to Austin would make things easier for Greg, and I would have less time alone since he was still volunteer coaching for the Texas Longhorns. The kids seemed to be okay with another big move, especially Hayley, who was having a hard time adjusting to high school in Arizona. The Austin vibe was much more to her liking.

Maybe because the younger girls had each other, it was easier for them to adjust to new situations and places. As for Dawson, he surprisingly went with the flow, and I quickly got to work gathering together his team of therapists once again. Finding a good therapist is like finding the perfect soul mate, there has to be a mutual trust and connection. It's either there that first meeting or it's not.

This is when Olivia came into our lives. She would remain one of Dawson's main caregivers and a part of our family for many years to follow. She had a quiet, calm demeanor, and the moment she would walk in the door, I instantly felt better just knowing she was there. She pushed Dawson, but never in the harsh or brutal way that he had experienced in the past. Her love and patience, along with her dedication to finding ways to make the tiniest of breakthroughs, shaped Dawson into the person he is today. He is potty trained because of her, can sit in a restaurant because of her, and can follow simple tasks that used to be nearly impossible, because of her. All because she believed in him and never gave up. She would selflessly take him to her home for sleepovers to give us breaks, even after her own long day. She rescued me when I had strep throat and could not get off the couch. She saw our family at its very best and at its demoralizing worst, without judgment.

Dawson's occupational therapist, Angie, also came into our lives around this time and played a pivotal role in his progress over the years. Just like Olivia, she never gave up on him. She was always looking for new and creative ways to make his very complicated body physically stronger and less disorganized. She had an infectious smile, gorgeous green eyes, and a kindness about her that instantly made everything seem not so shitty. I have never seen someone commit so dutifully to teaching a child to ride a bike with training wheels in the steamy, humid

Texas summer heat as Angie, excitedly cheering for him as if he was her very own. Since Dawson is completely nonverbal, getting through to him can be extremely challenging. His therapists and caregivers never gave up trying new ways to reach him. They had more patience than I could ever dream of having.

Angie also had a son with autism, so she understood all the ups and downs that came with having a special child. This gave me the feeling that we were a family, in a way. I remember us laughing hysterically one day as we shared poop stories about our sons—how many people can you have that conversation with? She was there with open arms when the tears would come, which happened often during the years she helped Dawson. Like Olivia, she saw the beautiful sides to my family, along with some of the worst, without showing any kind of judgement, and never pulled away from us. Evidence once again that there are true angels on this earth.

Shortly after we settled back in Austin, Greg and I separated for the second time. Again, I cannot tell you what sparked Greg to pack the *bye-bye bag*. I can't recall one specific argument, but this time Greg got an apartment and was there for a quite a while. I really don't remember much about that chapter of *Crazy Town*. I was confused, feeling both relief and sadness that he was gone. There was so much tension between all of us at that point, that it felt good to not be constantly walking on emotional eggshells. I remember feeling like I could suddenly breathe and laugh with the girls again. It was like a giant, long exhale that desperately needed to come out.

The "naughty burglar" thing, as we called it, was also in full swing between Greg and me during this long separation. All the kids would be in bed, then around 10:30 p.m., at least three nights a week, I would hear tapping on the French doors outside my bedroom. I would instantly feel an intense rush of excitement to feel his closeness. It was a strange and indescribable comfort. There was literally a physical reaction when we would get together; it made no difference whether or not we were on speaking terms. I don't have a word to explain it, other than pure chemistry, plain and simple. It is a real thing, folks, and if you have never felt it, you need to go find it because there is nothing else like it.

On the nights when we would meet during our separation, a word would hardly be said, and we would get right to the task at hand. Those times go down in history as the most exhilarating and satisfying sex we've ever had. He would then quietly slip out into the night without the kids even knowing he had been there, back to his apartment downtown. I remember wondering if other couples did the same thing during a separation; I am pretty sure the answer is a big No. It's a chemistry I tried really hard to duplicate in other relationships (maybe a little too hard) and honestly never could.

Greg eventually came back home again, and we vowed to work harder on our relationship. Our circle of friends was starting to expand in Austin, and, looking back, it was a crazy, chaotic time. Some of our couple-friends were normal and happy, while others lived on the edge with clear volatility in their marriages. Some of the husbands got along and some didn't, but for the most part, all the wives enjoyed each other. There were many Girls Night Out evenings, and we would come up with any reason we could find to have Happy Hour.

As the months passed, a smaller group of girls started to form, and with these girls, there was no question we were probably going out more than we should. Sometimes it felt like we were crazed, hormonal teenage girls looking for the nearest keg party. But in reality we were just a group of middle-aged moms sharing wine and laughing about life. It felt so different than being at home, with all the doom and gloom of my life there. When I was with my friends, I forgot all about the sadness and was a normal woman, just like them, even if it was just for a couple of hours. But something bad was in the air, and I don't think I was the only one who noticed.

I soon became extremely close with Amanda. I liked her instantly. Her husband had a lot in common with Greg, and we all became fast friends. Amanda had this *thing* about her: She was magnetic and had a way of making you feel like you were the most important thing to her when she wanted to. She would constantly tell you how beautiful or how amazing you were, along with everything else you would want to hear about yourself. She was stunningly gorgeous and would turn heads wherever we went. I envied how she carried herself, like she didn't have a care in the world. She had a curvaceous, athletic yet feminine figure, long golden-brown hair, and an infectious smile. She had the kind of beauty that looked flawless without a stitch of makeup, wearing a baseball hat, side braids and ripped-up jeans. Most of all, she always had the perfect golden tan to match her golden hair, thanks to the tanning salon membership she used probably more than was good for her.

Everyone seemed to be drawn to her, especially men. I would just sit back in a bar or restaurant and watch in awe as she would work a male bartender or waiter into thinking she was truly interested in him. She had her flirt down pat and would turn any man into mush just by flashing her Farrah Fawcett smile and giving them her undivided attention. Her husband Dave was no slouch either. They were pretty much the most gorgeous couple in Austin, if you ask me. Dave was quiet and a bit shy, but tall, with boyish good looks and a body to go along with it. Their personalities could not have been more opposite, and I noticed when he sometimes seemed uncomfortable with her outgoing behavior but would just sit back, smile, and lovingly shake his head.

They had numerous get-togethers at their sprawling white Texas stone house, hosting dinners and game nights that everyone wanted to be invited to. Greg and I were actually in a pretty good place at this point, at least I felt we were. We had committed to our marriage and promised each other there would be no more separating when things got tough. We said we were going to talk more and not shove things under the rug. It felt nice to be confident that all was going to be okay with us and that maybe the worst was over—we would get through this together.

WHEN A MARRIAGE STARTS TO CRACK from lack of respect, bad things can, and will, happen. Those ugly cracks only give trouble a free pass to slide right in, sometimes unnoticed.

The flirtation between Amanda and Greg was very subtle at first, then it became curiously obvious enough for me to ask a few friends if they'd noticed anything. Some said Yes, and some said there was no way either of them would do anything to hurt me. What kept nagging at me was that I had witnessed how Amanda could put a spell on men, especially vulnerable men. Greg and I had our troubles in the past, but now we were working on our relationship, and we were moving on. I was committed to making it work, and I wanted to make sure Greg knew how much I loved him. I was confident we were going to be fine. But I soon started to feel like I was the only one working on our marriage.

Looking back, there were signs of impending trouble. They were so small, yet blinking lights, right in front of my eyes. One day Greg told me he wanted to go to the UT football game with Amanda and Dave. Greg knew I couldn't go because we would not be able to get a sitter for Dawson on such short notice. I told him I thought it was a little strange to go with just them. We didn't have a fight about it, but I knew he could tell I didn't like the idea. He went anyway.

About thirty minutes later, he walked back into the house, took me in his arms and cried. He apologized profusely, said he felt horrible about the whole thing. It was so bizarre that he would cry about something so small and feel bad about something I wasn't all that upset about. Now I know it was his guilty conscience messing with his head. There was that fleeting moment when he decided to come home instead of going to the game with them. He was feeling guilty about something, but what about, I did not know yet.

Shortly after that incident, I had arranged for us to have dinner with Amanda and Dave at our favorite Mexican restaurant. I had just gotten off the phone with Amanda, when Greg came in the back door happy and in an exceptionally good mood.

I told him about the dinner plans and he said, "Yes, I know." What? I vividly remember thinking, How did he know about this already? When I asked him how he knew about our dinner plans, he stammered and made up something that really didn't make sense, but I just blew it off.

The signs continued. He started wearing cologne every day and had a little spring in his step that had not been there in quite a while. I was either too busy to really worry about it, or my subconscious didn't want to see it.

Amanda was even more over-the-top nice to me during this time, and we saw each other almost daily. She confided in me about everything, from her own marriage issues to probing me for information about mine. When I saw her, she would tell me how much she loved me and how I was like a sister to her. I loved her like a sister as well.

The night the four of us went to dinner at that Mexican restaurant changed the path of so many lives. On the way home from dinner, I confronted Greg about Amanda being just a little too friendly, in a flirtatious way, during dinner and acting bizarrely giddy. I was just getting over the flu, so I was the only one not drinking as they were pounding shots of tequila. I saw everything with crystal-clear eyes. Greg got extremely defensive about my observation as we pulled into the garage, and made me feel horrible for even asking about such craziness. He even raised his voice to me . . . that never happened.

Greg got out of the car once things cooled down a little bit, and went inside the house. I was going to meet Amanda halfway between our houses since Brenna, who was now fourteen, was babysitting her kids. Amanda suggested we meet halfway so I didn't have to make the full twenty-minute drive to come get Brenna. When we met in the parking lot, I confided in her about how Greg was acting strange and that we got in a little argument on the way home, but I didn't tell her what it was about. She told me she and Dave got in a fight as well, and we chatted about that for a minute before we hugged each other and said goodbye. She gave Brenna a big bear hug in true Amanda loving fashion, thanked her for watching the kids, and we drove away.

All the way home, I was convinced Greg would welcome me with a heartfelt apology for overreacting the way he did and all would be smoothed over. But that is far from what happened.

When I got home, Greg was already asleep and snoring loudly; so much for that apology. I was exhausted from the evening and from Dawson being up so much the night before, so I decided to sleep in the guest room—something I rarely did. I knew a good night's sleep and a sober husband would make the whole strange situation better, and we would laugh about it later.

When I woke up the next morning, Greg was gone. There was a note on the desk saying how he did not appreciate my accusations about him and Amanda, and he needed to cool off at a friend's house. It wasn't even a big enough fight to cool off from, and I was suddenly very confused. How did he leave the house without me hearing him or the garage door opening? Most importantly, when did he leave? He was sound asleep when I went to bed well after 10:30 p.m. It was completely out of character for him to just leave in the night, and a strange sense of panic filled my head.

I had plans to hold an open house for a new listing later that day, and Greg was still not home by the time I needed to leave. I was irritated that he had forgotten about watching Dawson, and now had to ask one of our daughters to be in charge, which I hated doing. I texted him before I left but he did not respond, so I figured he was sleeping it off, enjoying the quiet at his friend's house, which only annoyed me even more. I would have given anything for a full night's sleep, and was now starting to get officially angry.

A few weeks earlier, Amanda had mentioned that they wanted to sell their big house and get something a little smaller. I texted her and told her she should come to see the cute house I was holding open that day, thinking it would be perfect for their family. An hour later she showed up at the open house. The first thing I thought when I saw her was how disheveled she looked. She was in a frenzied mood, with wide animated eyes as she spoke to me. She went on to describe the fight she'd had with Dave, and I told her how Greg had actually left the house and I had not heard back from him yet.

We walked through the house, joking and laughing just like any other day, like best friends do.

"Oh my gosh, Greg would **LOVE** this giant mirror!" I said with a laugh when we got to the master bath. Greg always enjoyed a good mirror nearby during sex, and that was the first thing I thought of when I saw it. As soon as I said it, her face went as white as a sheet.

"What are you talking about?" she asked nervously.

"You know how Greg likes mirrors, silly. We just talked about that last week!"

She let out an awkward laugh, which made me laugh as well.

## Chapter 14

When she decided to head on out, she gave me a big hug goodbye, followed by the usual "I love you!" She flashed a big smile as she waved and climbed into her SUV.

When I got home, Greg was there. He looked like he had been up all night, not at all as rested as I had imagined he would be. I hugged him tightly, told him how sorry I was about the previous night and that I would not bring it up again. He didn't hug me back. Right then, I knew something was terribly wrong.

I started to feel horrible for thinking the things I had told him in the car the night before, and I could tell he was still mad. He didn't say much the rest of the day, and I decided I would not bring it up again.

That evening, we decided to meet a few couples at the golf club we belonged to for dinner, and I was relieved to think about a nice night out. It would be good for us to see friends, instead of giving each other the silent treatment all night at home. By the time we headed back to the house later that evening, all seemed to be fine between us, and I was feeling much better.

After we got ready for bed, I tried to initiate sex. It had been a little longer than usual since the last time, and it was sort of my non-verbal peace offering.

He took my hand off of his chest and said, "Not tonight." Another first.

"What is wrong, babe?" It sounded more like a plea than a question. I noticed he had a nervous sweat starting to form on his face.

"Nothing is wrong, I'm just tired and still a little hungover." He said it with a raspy voice that gave me a very uncomfortable feeling.

"I'm sorry, honey," he responded as he rolled over and went to sleep. I did the same, but my mind was going a hundred miles an hour as I lay wide awake.

At 4:30 a.m., I got out of bed with my head still racing. I noticed the light blinking on Greg's Blackberry charging by his sink, indicating there was a message. In all our years of marriage, I had never looked at his phone, but this time something was telling me to look at it. I swallowed down my feeling of guilt, picked up the phone and clicked.

*"I Love you more"* illuminated the screen. I blinked to clear my eyes. It was from Amanda.

I instantly felt a rush of dizziness, combined with the need to throw up. Were the words I was reading real? It was the only text that was there when I tried to scroll with trembling fingers. He was careful to delete his last text to Amanda, never thinking he wouldn't have the chance to delete her response in the morning. Greg had told her he loved her before he fell asleep next to me.

The night after the four of us left the Mexican restaurant, Amanda didn't sleep on her couch, and Greg didn't cool off at a friend's house. They both left their homes after their spouses had gone to sleep and went to a hotel for the night. It soon became clear why Amanda was disheveled the next day at the open house—she had come straight from the hotel to see me after spending the night with my husband. She actually acted as if it was just another day, pretending to be my best friend just hours after spending the entire night with Greg.

AFTER I READ THE TEXT, I started to tremble uncontrollably and the whole room felt like it was turning upside down. At first, I could not actually comprehend what I was reading, I was seeing the reality of my worst fear right in front of my eyes. I have never cried so violently since that day and hope I never will again. I'm positive I sounded like a wounded animal caught in a trap, because that is exactly what it felt like.

I walked over to Greg's side of the bed where he was still sleeping, sat him up, and slapped his face—hard. I had never slapped anyone in my entire life. My body just did it, involuntarily, without warning and without my consent. You can probably imagine the look of pure horror on his face, seeing his wife, or some version of her, leaning over him screaming and crying.

"I KNEW IT, I KNEW IT, I KNEW IT!" I cried, over and over again as he just sat there wide-eyed and stunned from the rude awakening of my slap. When he finally spoke, he acted like he had no idea what I was talking about and cooly told me to calm down.

"It was an 'I love you' like a brother and sister would say, NOT what you're thinking," he tried to explain.

But I knew better, and there was no denying it or convincing me otherwise. I said more curse words than I could count as I paced our bedroom floor with my face in my hands, crying uncontrollably.

"Get the fuck out of this house!" I managed to get out through the sobs. I could not bear to look at his face when I said it. I thought I actually might be sick to my stomach.

I don't remember if he packed a bag, but I do remember asking him, as he walked out the door, "Do you love her?"

He quietly and confidently, without much expression, turned to me and said, "Yes."

At that moment, my heart dropped to the floor like a lead weight. I felt dizzy with grief. Just like that, without any real warning, I knew we could never survive this. It was over. I knew I had just lost the love of my life and our family was broken beyond repair.

I instantly thought of our children still sleeping upstairs. It was only 5:00 a.m., and I was thankful that they did not hear a thing, shockingly enough. I felt a sudden panic about what to do next. I could barely hold my phone, I was shaking so much. It took me a few seconds to scroll through the phone numbers until I found Dave's. I must have called five times but he never picked up.

I then called my dear friend Christy. I was crying uncontrollably when she picked up. I tried to get the words out through my tears, and when I finally did, she immediately said she was on her way over. My next call was to my parents. In my attempt to explain what had happened, I am sure I wasn't making any sense so early in the morning. They were living in New Mexico at the time, and Mom said she would check on flights to come as fast as she could, knowing I was alone with the kids now.

Then, I called Amanda. Her voicemail came on instantly. Just hearing her voice made my stomach turn over with overwhelming nausea.

## Chapter 15

I am not sure how much time had passed before Dave called me back, but when he did, he said calmly and with very little emotion, "I had a feeling about this."

We talked for a while, and it was through our conversation that we realized they had been together the night the four of us had dinner. He said Amanda went to spend the night at a "friend's house," not on their sofa as she had told me. I told him Greg had said he also went to a friend's house, so it didn't take much to put two and two together.

I was so grateful when Christy got to my house, I literally fell into her arms as she cried her own tears with me. I'll never forget how she came to my rescue on that early morning. In the days that followed, she checked in on me, put sticky notes with encouraging words all over my house and just sat and cried with me without saying a single word. Christy was not the only friend who showed love and support for me during those really dark days. The most amazing part of having girl friends is that they will drop whatever they are doing when one of their own is hurting or needs help. They really stepped up to the plate for me. At least most of them did.

Sometime after the sun came up, I received a text from Amanda. I wish so badly that I had saved that text, because it painted the perfect picture of how manic she was in trying to deny what had happened. She even suggested that I was the one with the problem, for thinking such horrible things. She told me that she loved Greg like a brother, trying to explain the "I love you more" text, just like Greg had told me a few hours earlier.

I immediately thought they must have conjured up the story together of what they were planning on telling me, because they were saying the exact same thing.

"I would never, ever, do anything like that to you, Sarah!" She was panicking now, with a pleading tone to her voice when she finally called me.

"You are like a sister to me—I only love Greg like a brother. You have to believe me," she said over and over again. As much as I wanted to believe the words coming out of her mouth, I knew for certain she was lying. I hung up. I couldn't breathe, much less talk to the person who had just destroyed my family.

One of the hardest parts of the whole mess was that it was Thanksgiving break and school was out. When the kids all woke up, they sensed something was very wrong. I wish now that I had never told them what had happened, but there was no hiding the pain I was in, and no lie seemed to make enough sense to tell them. I figured they were going to find out anyway, but I wish they had not been so young, especially Sophia and Brenna, who were twelve and fourteen at the time.

Hayley was a freshman at The University of Texas and quickly came to the rescue for me, as well as her siblings. There are not enough words to describe the amazing strength Hayley showed during that time. I can't imagine how hard it must have been for her, but she stepped up nonetheless, making sure that I was okay, and helping with the kids, especially Dawson. I tried so hard to keep it together for Brenna and Sophia. I am not sure if they really understood what had happened or how seriously it would eventually affect our family.

The day after it all came out, I took Brenna and Sophia to lunch, while Hayley stayed at home with Dawson. I wanted to pretend, as best I could, that we would carry on as usual. Unfortunately, it would prove to be an impossible task.

"Mom, I knew something was going on. I could see how Dad and Miss Amanda were always looking at each other," Brenna said bravely on the way home, in a quiet, caring voice.

I immediately started to cry. I cried that my children were now learning firsthand how horrible people can be, how friendships can mean nothing, and most of all, how their dad could hurt us so much.

I had no way of explaining any of it to them, because I could not make sense of it myself.

"I'm so sorry you girls have to go through this. I wish I could make it go away," I said as I wiped away my tears. "Let's just enjoy our hour out of the house, okay?" It came out in more of a begging tone than a comforting one. I was so tired of talking about it, because talking about it made me think about it, and thinking about it was unbearable. But it was only the beginning and impossible to pretend it never happened.

In our group of friends, it was like an atomic bomb had gone off. Bodies were scattered everywhere, and friendships were being torn in all directions, trying to figure out what had happened to our tight-knit group. For a few days, Greg stuck to his story that nothing was going on, while Amanda worked on trying to get our friends to believe her. She tried to get them to believe that she would never do anything like that, and some chose to believe her.

Finally, after a couple of days, Greg came by the house to get a few things. I had not seen him since that night, and I started shaking when his car pulled into the driveway.

*Did they do things in his car? Did she ever sit on my side in the passenger seat? Did anyone ever see them together in his car?* These random and yet relevant thoughts raced through my head. He walked inside looking more tired than I had ever seen him before. All the kids were sitting silently in the kitchen, and none of them got up to great him when he came in. We were all expressionless. We looked at him as if we didn't know who he was anymore; maybe we didn't.

For the first time in days, I was not crying. I walked over to him, took his face into my hands and begged him to tell me the truth.

"Zeke, if you have ever loved me, you will tell me the truth and put me out of my misery. I feel like I am going crazy and can't take the lies anymore . . . please," I pleaded.

With tears in his eyes, he confessed. It may sound crazy, but I felt a moment of gratitude toward him for putting me out of my misery. I wouldn't have to think I was crazy anymore. My brain could not take it any longer, and now I could start the process of dealing with all that had happened, and why.

The game was officially over after Hayley and I found the hotel they had stayed at through phone records and fake phone calls Hayley made to various hotels listed on the records. Apparently, Austin was very busy that night and most hotels were booked, which is why the phone records showed back-to-back calls around 11:30 p.m.

To find the right one, Hayley called each hotel, saying she had left some jewelry there under the name Amanda or Greg on the reservation. The last number she tried was the one.

Hayley hung up as soon as she heard the desk clerk say, "Yes ma'am, we do see you were here that night. Let me take a look in Lost and Found." I could tell in her eyes when she hung up that she had the truth I still did not want to believe. It took a few years to not cringe every time I drove by that hotel.

The weeks that followed were hazy at best. Hayley spent her entire break by my side, helping with the kids and household stuff. Friends came over to try and make me laugh, or sit with me while I cried. Even after the truth came out, a couple of friends decided to support Amanda, which hurt tremendously at first, but later turned out to be the best friend-weeding-out-process ever.

Greg begged to come home and swore it was over with Amanda. But after checking the phone records again, I could see they were still in constant contact. I was done and I was filing for divorce. The images of my best friend and my husband haunted me. I knew I could never trust Greg, let alone let him touch me, ever again. I could not even bear to drive by that Mexican restaurant for the longest time without feeling physically ill. How could I ever work through something like this? How could anyone?

At the time, I did not believe any counselor could help us or take away what was embedded in my brain, and honestly, I didn't have the energy to even try. I thought that if it had been a one-night stand with a stranger, maybe I could have worked through it. But this was my friend's face in my head, not a stranger's. My friend's body tangled up with my husband's body in the heat of passion. It was emblazoned in my head now and haunted my dreams. I knew I was not strong enough to forget it.

Maybe we just were not meant for each other after all. Maybe true love doesn't exist like I thought, and maybe I was easily replaceable by a woman like Amanda. Maybe they were meant for each other, and I was wrong for not nurturing my marriage enough. Maybe it was all my fault for allowing a friend like her in my life, and I had been interested in another man myself. I hated myself for ever wanting to be like her, or thinking she was so amazing and special. Maybe I was like her? I hated that thought more than anything.

Did I blame both of them? Hell yes, I did! But for some reason that I can't explain, I blamed her more. Yes, Greg was my husband, and he absolutely owned his part in all of it and was a willing participant. Trust me, I let him know many times in the years that followed how much he hurt me and our children. But she was my best friend and used everything I'd ever told her to make my husband think I didn't love him anymore, just so she could have him. She pretended to love my children as her own, completely manipulating what I thought was a very special friendship.

Yes, our marriage was struggling, but it was not up to her to end it for me. She used her sensuality and information against me to do just that. I still cling to the hope that she had some sort of personality disorder that was out of her control, and that she really was not aware of what she did to me. But honestly, I don't think I will ever know why she did what she did.

There were some days I thought maybe I deserved it for having my own thoughts of infidelity, but nobody deserves what I felt that morning—the ultimate betrayal from two people I loved at the exact same time.

IT IS HARD TO PUT INTO WORDS what the first year after the affair was like. Saying that it was a roller-coaster ride sounds a bit cliché, but that is exactly what it felt like. I had great days of feeling powerful and excited for the promise of all the newness coming my way, and extremely low days filled with sad reminders of all that had happened. I felt like the wind was knocked out of me if I ran into Amanda at the grocery store or at Starbucks; I would literally shake for hours. The images that I had worked so hard to get out of my head would all come flooding back, playing over and over in my head for days.

Greg moved back to Arizona for most of 2009 for a broadcasting job, an idea we were actually considering right before everything happened. But instead of us going together, he took a new girl he had started a relationship with. Hearing the news crushed me for the second time. I actually found out about the new love from a photo on our girls' computer. He had taken her along with our kids on a bowling date.

Once again, my need to be accepted by a man kicked into high gear. When your husband cheats on you, then runs off with a different girl entirely a month later, it is sort of hard not to take it personally. I had a constant feeling of self-doubt and low self-esteem that only the attention of a man would fill. I was a single mother of four, one of those with special needs. Who in the world was going to love me and all that came with it? I was damaged goods and had convinced myself I would be alone forever.

I was still plugging along, caring for Dawson's day-to-day needs and therapies, as well as three daughters with busy lives, trying the best I could to give them all the attention they needed. I felt as if I was in constant overdrive and tried to take breaks when I could. The girls were more than willing to help with Dawson now that they were old enough, but I hated to use them unless it was totally necessary, so I would go out after he went to bed. I slowly started getting serious about dating.

I won't make this portion of my life seem like it was all doom and gloom. Being single in your late thirties certainly isn't a terrible thing, especially loving love as much as I did.

It wasn't nearly as hard as I thought it would be to find someone interested in dating me. I really didn't have one certain type of man that I was attracted to; he just had to have a good sense of humor, be somewhat attractive, intelligent, above 6'1" and not broke. Good looks were important to me, but I could easily fall for a not-so-attractive guy with a fabulous personality easier than a guy that was drop-dead gorgeous without one. I actually steered clear of the guys who girls drooled over. I love confidence but detest arrogance to my very core. I found this type of man hard to trust—which was extremely important to me—and did not like feeling they were doing me a favor by being with them.

At one point, Kyle, my high school friend who I connected with while Greg and I were in the rough patch, tried to start a real relationship. As much as I loved and adored him—he was probably a perfect match for me—I just could not get there romantically. Maybe it was because I did care for him so much, that I wanted to spare him any of my emotional weirdness. It just felt strange for some reason.

## Chapter 16

I soon discovered the wonderful world of online dating. After the kids would go to bed, I loved perusing through *Match.com* in my pajamas with a bottle of wine and a bowl of popcorn. Thankfully this was before Bumble and other "swipe" dating sites, because that could have been deadly to a person like me!

Dating sites were so much easier and better than getting a baby-sitter or sitting in a bar, waiting for Mr. Right to come along. Don't get me wrong, I loved Happy Hour with my girlfriends as much as anyone, and loved it when interested men would join us at whatever high-top table we were gathered around. But it was more interesting to me when I could read all about the faces on the screen, their likes and dislikes, what they did for a living, where they had traveled, and their idea of the perfect date. It felt like Build-A-Bear, but with men instead of stuffed animals. It took me away from the stress of being a single parent or after a difficult day with Dawson. It made me feel like a desirable woman when men would reach out to me after seeing my profile. I thrived on reading all the nice things they would say about me without even meeting me in person. It was a rush I looked forward to almost every night.

I had pretty good success with dating sites. I would actually become engaged to one man, and married to another who I'd met online in the years that followed. Is that considered success, even though they didn't work out? I am not really sure how to answer that, but I still believe in the process. Many of my friends have met wonderful people online and are in very happy relationships.

I enjoyed the anticipation of going on a first date, wondering if their picture matched their profile and what their personality was like. I have always loved meeting new people and getting to know all about a perfect stranger, even when I knew within the first thirty seconds it was not going to be a love connection. I enjoyed dressing up and having an adult conversation. I knew that I probably didn't look good on paper, but for the most part, they didn't seem to mind about my past or that I had four children.

It was sometimes difficult telling someone new about Dawson and his autism. I needed them to understand that it was an important part of who I was and that Dawson would always be the main man in my life. Surprisingly, almost every man I told didn't seem to have a problem with it. They were actually very kind and curious about what Dawson was like and would ask me questions about him.

Dawson's autism was so profound, he really did not seem to notice anything was different at home or that Dad was even gone. His behavior stayed the same. He was still locked in his own world, and we still were trying to get in there to understand it. I was grateful the divorce had not impacted him, but worried a little that my girls' happy disposition was just a mask for how they really felt about everything, including me dating so quickly after what happened with their dad. I was probably gone at night more than I should have been. For me, a night out was my therapy for dealing with all the fear and shame I felt.

Dating in your thirties naturally produces stories, and I had my fair share. There were times while on a date when I would become speechless after a comment or shocked at how they looked nothing like their photo. My biggest pet peeve was when they would not be truthful about their height, which was as important to me as having eyes. Did they think I would not notice that they were looking up to me as we said hello for the first time? If they would lie about something as obvious as that, I would not be sticking around to find out what else they were willing to lie about.

My single friends and I had nicknames for some to keep them all straight, as we shared our battle stories. There was Bad Breath Bob, Loud Talker Larry, Awkward Andy, and my favorite, Sloppy

# Chapter 16

Steve—after my whole face got wet after a first, and last, makeout session. I had one guy tell me, the minute I sat down next to him at a bar table, that I would be so much prettier if I had long hair, but that my big boobs made up for it. Check, please!

Only once did I feel like I was in a really bad situation. After dinner with a guy who I had been out with a few times, we went back to his house. I thought I knew him well enough at that point to join him for one more drink before heading home. A few minutes after we got there, he became upset with me because I had no intention of sleeping with him. He'd had quite a few more drinks than I had, and I could see the frustration brewing in his intoxicated eyes.

"Take your clothes off and get in bed," he snarled as he threw a toothbrush at me; literally threw a toothbrush that hit my body, *super* romantic. I quickly realized the situation was going bad by the look of anger in his eyes. He seemed to be on a mission to get me into bed, and I no longer felt comfortable. Did I really know this guy and what he was capable of? I decided the answer was no.

I quickly said, "I really need to get home, I have an early wake-up call tomorrow to get kids off for school. Give me your address and I will call a cab, no need to drive me home." I realized this was the same feeling I'd had years ago in high school, and I didn't like it one bit.

This was before Uber, and I had trouble finding the number for a cab on my phone because I was shaking so much.

"What is the address here?" I asked when I finally got a cab company on the line.

"You figure it out," he snapped, as he went to his bedroom and slammed the door like an angry twelve-year-old. I found his address on a bill that was on the counter and went outside to sit on the front steps and wait for the cab. As I sat waiting, I started crying. I realized it was both humiliation and fear, but why I would feel that way for doing nothing wrong? Greg actually knew this guy from college. I wanted to tell Greg what had just happened and hear his comforting voice. I dialed his number and I told him everything. He was beyond angry, he wanted to come kick the guy's ass for doing that to me. And I loved that he wanted to.

CHAPTER 17

Shortly after Greg and I divorced in 2009, my friend Christy and I took a trip to Los Angeles after buying a charity fundraiser auction item to attend the *Ellen Degeneres Show*. Ellen's show literally saved my life during those first few difficult months. Many times I found myself laughing through tears while I watched. I was so excited to get away for a few days, a much-needed break from all my responsibilities at home.

As Christy and I waited in a large room with the other 300+ guests, the producers went around the room picking out about twenty of us, including Christy and me. After being asked a few questions about ourselves, we were then narrowed down to about eight ladies, and I was one of them. I was practically jumping out of my skin with excitement as we were told that five of us would be selected to participate in a game on stage for the chance to win a car later in the week. If you are an Ellen fan, you know exactly what I am talking about, and probably excited for me right now!

Our small group was taken to a trailer behind the studio, and the producers asked us to pretend what we would do if we heard our name being called from the audience. We took turns jumping around and clapping our hands like wild lunatics as the producer called out our names. My acting skills from my teen years kicked into high gear—I was determined to get on that stage.

The show began, and tears of joy welled up in my eyes as Ellen walked on stage. She was the only person who could bring a smile to my face for a long time, and there she was, right in front of me. After Ellen's opening monologue, they started calling the names one by one. Those called would be playing Blindfolded Musical Chairs, my all-time favorite Ellen game! My name was the third one called! I didn't have to use my acting skills at all by this point, as adrenaline completely took over. I don't think I have ever been more excited about anything in my life than I was when I heard my name called. Even though they said "Swindle" instead of "Swindell," I leapt from my seat and sprinted down the stairs to the stage so fast, I can't believe I didn't tumble down. I jumped around clapping frantically and hugging the other girls. Just then, a curtain opened and the new car was revealed. That escalated our excitement even more, if that was possible.

I ended up winning the game, and to this day can't remember the last time I had that much fun. I was invited back the following week to play in the finale for the chance to win the car, along with the other winners from the week before. Sadly, I didn't end up winning that red Ford Focus, but the experience goes on my Top 5 List of all-time favorite life moments:

1. Marrying Greg
2. The birth of my children
3. The World Series win
4. Hanging out with Garth Brooks and Trisha Yearwood and Trisha cooking us breakfast
5. Being on the *Ellen Degeneres Show*

Meeting Ellen and being on her show wasn't the only memorable part of that trip. After the show, Christy and I hit all the hot spots in L.A. and soaked up every minute of our trip. On the last night, we went to a new club that was a known hangout for celebrities. We were on a mission to catch a glimpse of whoever we could. There was a long line at the entrance that consisted of only the most beautiful people, and it was a little on the intimidating side. Christy and I attempted the old "flirt with the door guy" trick to avoid waiting in the mile-long line, and it worked! The tall and extremely hot man attending the door immediately sparked my attention. He had a John Mayer look to him, a look I usually am not attracted to, but I was that night.

He softly shook my hand with an intense and very interested look in his eyes and asked, "What is your name, beautiful?"

"Samantha." For some silly reason, I gave him a fake one. Maybe I was trying to be mysterious, which makes me laugh, even writing this, because I am about the most un-mysterious person around.

"I'm Derek, nice to meet you." Our hands lingered just a little longer than was necessary, but I didn't mind. I reluctantly let go, but not before giving him the best flirty smile I could produce.

As we got drinks at the bar and soaked up the energy around us, I noticed Derek staring at me. He couldn't leave his busy post at the entrance but motioned for me to come over to him, and I shyly obliged. As I approached, he looked at me like a tiger about to eat a steak dinner.

"You are absolutely gorgeous. Please tell me you are from here." I have always been a sucker for verbal affirmation, especially after all that I had been through, and his affirmation was incredibly intoxicating, even more so than my glass of wine.

We chatted for a few minutes about where I lived, why I was in L.A. and if I was married. Then out of the blue, he asked if he could kiss me. I have always been a fan of making out and sometimes even prefer just doing that to having sex. Much safer, fewer strings attached, and just as fulfilling for me.

"I think I might be a little old for you," I said, knowing he didn't care how old I was.

"You are the perfect age for me, and I have been dying to kiss you all night."

I wasn't married or even in a relationship at the time. I guessed that he could not be older than twenty-seven and later found out he was twenty-six. I told him I was thirty-nine, and his only response was that it made me even sexier. That was good enough for me!

We stood there making out like teenagers for a while, only stopping so he could let more people in the club when others would leave. Did I feel awkward making out with a total stranger in front of other total strangers? Not a bit. I was in another state, nobody knew who I was, and I could be anyone but a divorced mother of four. Samantha was living up to her fake name with pleasure.

"Okay, lovebirds, time to go," Christy said playfully as she grabbed my hand to leave. But not before Derek asked for my phone number and hoped we could stay in touch. Not expecting to hear from him again, I gave it to him.

Not long after the weekend in L.A., I decided to take a trip by myself to Laguna Beach. I wanted to see an old friend of mine from the Minnesota Twins days who was living in Orange County, and I welcomed spending a few days alone. I booked a beautiful oceanfront room at Surf and Sand Resort and was ready for a few days by myself with a good book, walks on the beach, and room service on my patio. I have always liked doing things by myself, which is odd, now that I think about how often I felt lonely for a man in my life. I happily go to movies alone, will sit alone in a restaurant, and highly recommend that every mother in the world take a three-day vacation completely alone. It is food for the soul.

I landed at LAX and secured a cab, heading south on Pacific Coast Highway to Laguna Beach. I was completely relaxed, happy to leave my very complicated life in Austin behind for a few days. Derek and I had been texting on and off since my last visit, and we had set a day for him to meet me at my hotel. Was I nervous or scared that a twenty-six-year-old total stranger was going to be *my* booty call? Nope, not in the slightest. I checked in, unpacked and got ready for my "date."

I met him in the lobby, and for a fleeting moment I thought he should be dating my oldest daughter, not about to hook up with her mother. My first thought was that he looked so much more age appropriate the night at the club, wearing a suit, than he did in his board shorts, a tank top and tousled dark hair. I had forgotten how tall he was, he had to have been at least 6'4", which is exactly what I liked since I'm so tall. We had a quick and nervous kiss hello, then without saying a word, I took his hand and led him directly to the elevator. My heart was pounding so hard, I was convinced he could hear it. Nothing about this was normal for me, but I was not turning back now.

We walked down the long outdoor hallway overlooking the ocean to my suite. When I opened the door, he commented on how nice my room was as I opened two cold beers that I had waiting. I have always been more of a wine drinker, but assumed my younger companion would prefer beer. I needed something to calm the nerves that had suddenly taken over my entire body, and to keep myself from calling the whole crazy thing off.

We talked for a few minutes as we sat in chairs opposite each other, about the book I was reading, the weather outside, and what my plans were for the remainder of my trip. Our age difference was suddenly very apparent, showing how difficult it was to carry on a meaningful conversation. But then again, I guess we were not really there to have a heated discussion about politics or the latest mortgage crisis sweeping the nation. After our poor attempt at small talk, he stood up and held his hand out to me. This was happening, and I was terrified and exhilarated all at the same time.

Being that I love my family with all my heart, and I will look them in the eye every day after this book is published, I will leave those details out. Derek was exactly what this broken, exhausted woman needed at that exact moment in her life. I felt cherished, appreciated, and worshipped in a very dramatic-sounding way. It was the best remedy for me to feel alive again. He had awakened parts of my body that had been asleep for much too long. He allowed me to forget about the pain of autism, of being a single mom, and that I was the girl who was cheated on by her husband. We stayed in touch for a while, but honestly, that one day was all I needed.

I hope every woman in the world who has ever felt the way I did, finds her own Derek to come to the rescue. To treat her like she is the most amazingly beautiful human being on earth. That is exactly what he did for me, and for that I will be forever grateful.

I MET SHANE A FEW MONTHS after my Laguna Beach trip. He was a welcome ray of sunshine and one who I had never experienced in a male personality. He was the complete opposite of Greg in every way, which was just what I probably needed. He was tall, with green eyes and sandy-blond curly hair that I could not stop running my fingers through. He had a slim athletic build and a big personality to go with it. He had two children who were ten and thirteen and who enjoyed hanging out with my kids, especially Brenna and Sophia, who were closer in age. They were sweet kids and easy to like from the very beginning.

He made me laugh constantly with his goofy and sometimes outrageous comments and impersonations. Things progressed quickly, and we saw each other almost every day. He was thoughtful and involved with all my kids and was genuinely interested in what was going on in their lives, especially Dawson. He would even clean up after Dawson when he would have a poop accident in the bathtub, which happened almost nightly. Not an easy task for anyone's stomach to handle, much less a non-family member. His extended family welcomed us with open arms, included us in family get-togethers, and I loved how close they all were. Shane was my first real boyfriend who took my mind off all that had happened in the past. I soon found out his wife had cheated on him as well. We had something in common, something that most people can't comprehend, and it bonded us in a way that made me feel safe. Something I definitely needed at the time.

Christmas Eve 2009, a few months after we'd met, Shane proposed. With all six kids standing around him as he bent on one knee holding a beautiful diamond ring. Everyone was gathered in my kitchen, all with tears of joy in their eyes.

I said "Yes!" as all the kids jumped around, hugging each other with excitement. Even with all the joy and laughter going on around me, I had a strange feeling that I could not quite understand.

It was almost exactly one year after my life had imploded, and everything seemed to be taking a turn for the better, but it was Greg's face I saw momentarily after that proposal—just like in the movie *The Notebook*. I wrote it off as being a natural feeling after being married for almost seventeen years, and I knew it would still take some time to fully recover. I truly believed I was in love again and was excited about my new future with my new soon-to-be blended family. We decided to plan the wedding sooner than later for reasons I really can't remember now, other than we were just anxious to get this party started, and his lease was almost up on his rental house.

I am really good at moving, and soon I discovered that I am also really good at planning a wedding in less than four months. Everyone was so excited for the big day, including me and all the kids. I was also busy getting my home ready for three more people to move in. I was sure it was the best thing for my children, and I was ready to have the feeling of being a whole family again.

I had pretty much been married my whole life, since I was eighteen. It was all I really knew, and being someone's wife was where I felt at ease. I was not alone anymore and it felt good. But that warm fuzzy feeling didn't last long, and as the date got closer, panic set in.

# Chapter 18

The wedding was just around the corner, and I tried with all my heart to keep that panic tucked deep inside, knowing if I called the whole thing off, the kids would be heartbroken.

I vividly remember Shane and me getting into our first major fight the day they were moving into my house. I am sure I was being a total bitch, but the mess that was forming all over the house was testing every agitated nerve in my body. I always kept my house very clean and organized, and all of a sudden there were kids running everywhere, half-drank soda cans, water bottles, and random shoes all over the place.

At one point I firmly asked all the children that had taken over my home, "Is it possible to NOT eat or drink something for more than five minutes?" as I snatched up more chip bags and half-drank water bottles from the coffee table. To this very day, I don't have water bottles in my house.

Shane thought it would be fun to invite his kids' friends over during the move-in process, but the loud commotion of kids running up and down the stairs and slamming doors felt as though a bomb in my brain was about to go off any second. Dawson was not having a good day, either, and the commotion seemed to be getting to him as much as it was getting to me. I had finally reached my breaking point, and I let Shane know exactly how I was feeling.

I was bawling my eyes out, and from the look on his face, I think he was actually scared. I could not tell if he was in shock from me crying so hard, or if it was something else. He asked me if I wanted to call the whole thing off, and while a tiny voice deep inside screamed "YES," my outside voice quietly said "No."

The wedding was a week away. I had paid for the entire $45,000 affair myself, and the kids would have been crushed if I called it off. I wrote off the whole episode to nerves, being tired, and the strangeness of a new man living in the same house and sleeping in the same bed that Greg and I had shared just one year earlier.

Despite my mental breakdown the week before, the rehearsal dinner turned out to be a success. Everyone had a great time at the intimate little restaurant we had rented, and the bond between the families was easy to see. My family of four children was about to become six, and I had to admit it was sweet how they all got along so well, making everything seem okay.

"Picture perfect," I thought, as I tried to ignore the *"oh shit, what am I about to do?"* feeling enough to enjoy the evening with friends and family. To everyone watching, we were going to be a perfectly blended family, but inside my head, it looked very different.

When the dinner was over, Hayley and I climbed into my black SUV to head back to the resort where the wedding would take place. The younger ones were staying at the house with Shane and would be coming back bright and early the next morning for all the wedding-day preparations. I was happy the dinner went well, but I still had a nagging feeling, something I couldn't put my finger on. Maybe I was still tired from everyone moving into my house the week before, combined with Dawson trying to adjust to all the chaos, and keeping up with his therapies and his daily care. Or were all these strange feelings a reaction to the text I got from Greg earlier that day?

Greg texted that he was happy for me, but that he was heading to the liquor store to get a bottle of Grey Goose so he didn't have to think about me getting married. He said he missed me and hated what had happened between us. He wanted to make sure I was happy.

What did that mean, and why was I feeling a deep desire to run to Greg and tell him I was scared and that I still loved him?

Hayley and I drove to the hotel in silence for a few minutes, then it all came pouring out, like lava finally erupting from a volcano. She chose her words carefully at first, and I could tell she was trying to be as gentle with my feelings as possible. I knew where it was going, and I didn't want to hear one word of it. I was too scared to go there.

With her brown eyes pleading, she said, "Mom, please don't do this. You're not ready, you need more time to get over Dad. It's too soon, and I'm not sure any of this is right."

With the sudden sense that I needed to defend myself, I snapped back, "Are you serious? Why are you doing this to me now, of all times?"

Both of us were bawling as we drove up to the hotel, and it only got worse when we got back to the room we were sharing for the night. We went to bed still mad at each other, and with nothing solved after a long and tearful night of going back and forth.

Way down deep, I knew she was right, and that was the reason I was so defensive. Those were the same strange, nagging feelings I had been having for weeks. So many lives were about to be affected, and the responsibility of it all completely overwhelmed me. We woke up the next day after only a few hours of sleep, both with dark, puffy eyes that no amount of makeup was going to hide. Hayley was right, but it was too late to turn back now. The makeup and hair girls were knocking on the hotel room door.

CHAPTER 19

Shane and I lasted less than a year before divorcing. It was late 2010, and I felt humiliated, embarrassed and upset with myself for putting all the children through so much uncertainty and turmoil. I was constantly filled with confusing thoughts. When I told Greg during a phone conversation that I was unhappy with how things were going with Shane, and that I thought I'd made a huge mistake, I was completely taken aback when he told me he wasn't happy with his current girlfriend, Elaine, either.

Elaine was almost my twin. She looked so much like me that for months people thought Greg and I had gotten back together, thinking they were seeing us around town. She was shorter and had more of an athletic build than I, but we could easily pass for the same person.

The first time I met her, she and Greg were coming to pick up Dawson. She was a bit cold and didn't say much as she stood in the doorway of the home Greg and I had once shared together. I immediately noticed her Daisy Duke cut-off shorts, high-heeled wedges, and the muscular legs I always wished I had. My legs were long but definitely lacked in the muscle department. Yes, I was absolutely jealous.

The text I got from Greg the day before my wedding had really messed with my emotions and was in the back of my mind throughout much of my marriage to Shane; not where it should have been. I knew I should not be feeling the way I was feeling, and the guilt was tearing me up inside. Shane and his children deserved better than what I was giving. The day Greg told me he was not happy with Elaine was the day I knew I could not go on in my marriage. I was living a lie that I just could not cover up anymore.

I felt a sudden surge of happiness that maybe, just maybe, there was a chance for Greg and me after all. Did the conversation we had contribute to me wanting to leave Shane? It most certainly didn't help. Not only was I unhappy in my marriage, Greg was unhappy in his relationship as well. This made the choice to get out of my marriage clear; this was the nudge I needed.

This would be our first attempt at possibly getting back together. I didn't have a doubt in my mind at that time that we could and would make it work again, despite all the trauma that went down almost two years earlier. I missed Greg so much it was painful to even let myself feel it. I could not believe we were getting another chance to make it right again.

To compare the person I am in now in 2019 to the person I was in 2010, is to say that I am not even close to being the same woman. I remember thinking Greg and I were completely ready to put the past behind us and start fresh, as if nothing had ever happened, but nothing could have been farther from reality. I still had constant thoughts about Amanda, and the visions still raced in my head every time I closed my eyes.

I know I would have seriously benefited from talking to a therapist; but for some reason, I always thought I could handle it on my own, and it would eventually get better. All I wanted was to have my life back the way it was, and I vowed to never take my marriage to Greg for granted again. I was sure he would continue to apologize for what he had done until I felt safe again, and with a little more time, I would be able to completely trust him. Yes, I realize now how absolutely insane it was that I was willing to get back together with someone I still didn't trust, but that is what I thought. I wanted my family back more than anything in the world.

I remember it was right around Christmas when Greg and I decided to move forward with our plan. I told Hayley about it but didn't want to tell Brenna and Sophia just yet. Something told me to wait; I just wanted to protect them. I could tell that Hayley was a little apprehensive about the whole idea, and she warned me it was too soon for me to make any big decisions. As usual, though, I didn't want to hear anything that didn't correspond with what I wanted, and I wanted Greg more than anything else in the world. A very selfish way of thinking, especially being a mom.

Greg decided to write Elaine a letter and leave it on their kitchen counter before he left for a business trip to Arizona. (Letters are always a great way to break up with someone that you have been dating for a year and who had just moved into your place.) Since I was already in Arizona attending a funeral, it seemed like the perfect place to leave the past behind us and begin our new love story with a couple of days together in another state.

In a nutshell, Greg's letter explained to her that he was going back to his family and that he was very sorry. Obviously, that wasn't going to go over very well with Elaine and understandably so; but sadly, I didn't care. Greg had been mine for seventeen years, and she had only had him for one. In my head, the simple math made it all okay. I know it sounds completely heartless, and that's because it was.

I knew something was wrong when Greg arrived in Arizona and he didn't text or call me, nor did he respond to any of my attempts to reach him. My gut was twisted with anxiety. I was all too familiar with this feeling, and I knew deep inside it was not going to end well; at least for me it wouldn't.

I had imagined a beautiful, heartfelt night together in a hotel, spending the night wrapped in each other's arms, never wanting to let go. He would tell me over and over again how sorry he was for ever hurting me and how it was the biggest mistake of his life. We would make love and all would be forgiven and forgotten. We would get back home, sit the whole family down and surprise them with the news that Mom and Dad are getting back together and how sorry we were for the last two years of madness.

Unfortunately, my little fantasy didn't play out; not even close. I never heard from or saw Greg the entire time I was in Arizona, other than one short text saying he had made it there, but was busy. I was a mess the whole plane ride back to Austin. I cried on and off and tried to calm my nerves with wine, which seemed to only make the tears fall even more. I refused to allow myself to think he might be having second thoughts and continued to make up various reasons for his radio silence all the way home.

Once Greg was back in Austin, I could tell he was avoiding me as much as possible and making excuses for not seeing me in Arizona, but I tried to shove all the fear aside. It was Christmas Eve, and Greg was still planning on spending it with us, since apparently Elaine was gone. I spent all day getting the house perfect and prepared all his favorite foods just like in the past. I wanted the evening to remind him of how wonderful life used to be as a family. Even Dawson was in an exceptionally good mood that day.

I knew instinctively the moment he came in that something was very off and it was not going to go as planned. He was very quiet and seemed uncomfortable, which made us all feel the same. His face was pale, and he was not interested in any of the food I had made. He was not even interested in conversation with the girls.

# Chapter 19

Nothing about it felt good or natural, and it definitely didn't feel like Christmas Eve. I made the mistake of breaking out old family videos to lighten the mood, and while the kids enjoyed them, I could see in Greg's eyes he did not. I sat there watching as tears stung my eyes. I had cried so much by this point it almost felt natural when my eyes welled up once again. I ached for my old life playing on the TV screen and realized that my hope of that ever happening again might not happen after all. It scared me to death.

When the kids went to bed, Greg and I sat alone in the family room and had small talk. We talked about what was going on with the girls and how Dawson's therapies were going. I shared with him how rough the night before was and how I wished I could figure out what kept Dawson up all night. I was tired, but I didn't want Greg to leave.

"Would you like to stay and help me stuff stockings?" It sounded more like a desperate plea than a simple question.

He nervously said, "I better get going, but thanks."

I suddenly had that familiar sense that he was hiding something, and I felt nauseous. I could see on his face that he was changing his mind about all of it, but I was terrified to admit it to myself. He gave me a long hug goodbye, a hug that felt like it might be our last. There was no passionate kiss or suggestion that he might want to spend the night, as I had hoped.

As he left the house through the side door, he turned around one more time and waved to me as I stood in the doorway. I could have sworn I saw tears in his eyes just like mine, but his were not for the same reason.

CHAPTER 20

It was 4:00 a.m. on Christmas morning. I could tell by the loud noises coming from Dawson's room that he was up for the day and not because he was excited to tear open his presents from Santa. He didn't even know who Santa was. At almost ten years old, he never understood or was interested in anything that had to do with Christmas or any other special occasion. He never wanted to unwrap presents or blow out birthday candles. His only interest was to flap the ribbon used on the gifts or to occasionally smile at the birthday plate that sang the "Happy Birthday" song when you pushed the button. He always woke up at odd hours of the night, but when he woke up this late (early), he was up for the rest of the day with no chance of going back to sleep. Time for a car ride to let the rest of the kids sleep awhile longer.

I knew I was making a mistake the moment I exited the freeway and turned down the dimly lit street leading to Greg and Elaine's townhome. I typed in the gate code as Dawson loudly clapped in the back seat, enjoying an especially loud vocal outburst. As the gate swung open, my heart started pounding out of my chest and my mind was going a mile a minute. I felt sudden panic as I got closer to his unit, and then I saw it. Her car was parked in the driveway.

She was back. Now everything about Christmas Eve made sense. That was why he was so distant with me, why he didn't kiss me and why he didn't stay the night. He had gone back to her. He chose her over me. And once again, I felt my heart being ripped from my chest. For the second time he had picked another woman over me. Seeing her car parked in the driveway was almost as painful as reading that text two years ago, but at least I was less surprised, if that was even possible.

As I drove out of the gated community, I mistakenly allowed my brain to wander and imagine the two of them cuddling in bed or worse, doing other things. I was sure they were relieved to be back in each other's arms after a short breakup—a very short breakup—and she must have forgiven him for the Dear John letter he left in the kitchen the week before. I wondered if he had begged her to forgive him? Or did she beg for him to come back?

By the time I made it back to the freeway I was sobbing so hard that I could hardly see the road in front of me. Dawson was quiet, almost watching me with curiosity as to what was wrong with his mother.

I remember thinking, *I bet he wishes he could give me words of comfort or encouragement.* I would have given anything to hear him speak and say those words to me. Maybe just the way he had become quiet while I was having my mini breakdown was his way of showing his love; quietly comforting me the only way he could.

Somehow I pulled myself together enough to give my kids some kind of a normal Christmas morning. I didn't share that Elaine was back with Dad and that I saw her car there on a Dawson drive earlier that morning, but I am sure they could tell something was wrong. Once again, I felt defeated, and on top of that, I was ashamed that I had allowed myself to go there. I was absolutely at the very lowest point I had ever been in my life. I did not understand just how bad it was until years later, when I allowed myself to reflect on it.

# Chapter 20

It was not until I was on another Dawson drive in the middle of the night not long after the holidays in 2011 that I felt the urge to drive through the barrier on a tall overpass not far from my home. Dawson was having major ups and downs, and I could not seem to get his bowel disease under control. I was utterly exhausted from the lack of sleep, along with an overwhelming sense of defeat and sadness that I just could not seem to shake. I had honestly convinced myself that we would both be better off dead. At least Dawson's pain would stop, and he would not have autism in heaven. My girls would get a stepmother someday, probably Elaine, who would surely be more stable than I was, and they would be just fine. I even had the strange thought that because she looked like me, it would somehow be easier on the kids to adjust.

The night on the overpass is still very clear in my head, even though I wasn't thinking clearly at all. Dawson's yelling from the back seat that night, combined with the overwhelming feeling of despair, almost won the fight going on in my head. But something quieted the storm in that early-morning hour.

As someone who was never a part of organized religion, I believe it was absolutely a God moment for me. It's too hard to even think about all of the amazing things I would have missed—especially now that I am a grandmother—what a gift that I would have never experienced. I would have missed out on college graduations, my children's weddings, and even the simple joy of taking a walk in the sunshine. Someone upstairs had to have seen my future and knew I would be okay. That, and my love for my family kept me on the road and led me safely back home.

I do believe now that exhaustion played a major role in my mental well-being and contributed to me not thinking clearly. Years and years of hardly ever getting a full night's sleep finally caught up to me, and my world falling apart certainly did not help. It is why new mommies are always feeling as if they are in a fog from waking up with their new babies. My baby was now ten years old and still not sleeping through the night. That is a *very* long baby phase!

I wish everyone going through dark times were allowed just a tiny peek into the future and be able to see all the beautiful things in life that are ahead. I don't understand why I was so apprehensive about getting professional help or talking about all my feelings. It's interesting to me how I consider myself a private person when it comes to sharing my feelings, never wanting to tell a stranger who doesn't even know me, all my problems. Yet, I am eager to write an entire book and share it with the world now!

If you ever see someone who you think may be in a bad place or going through difficult personal times, reach out to them often. Even several times a day, if needed. Make them feel they are important to you, they are loved, and that they matter to you and to so many others. Reaching out and checking in on someone in need truly could mean the difference between life and death.

If you are the person who thinks ending your life is the answer, please don't be embarrassed or afraid to ask for help. I understand how dark life can feel and how incredibly real those feelings are. I was fortunate enough to work through those moments because people reminded me that I am loved in tiny little ways. You, too, are loved more than you will ever know.

CHAPTER 21

I CAN NEVER SAY ENOUGH about how my daughters supported me during all the ups and downs, especially when it came to how I was dealing with stress. I thought I was doing the best I could, but I know now that I absolutely could have done better.

As I mentioned at the beginning of the book, I don't want to assume what they might have been going through. They seemed to be doing totally fine from an outsider's perspective, but they were dealing with their own internal battles, while not verbally expressing it.

Hayley and I have always been like sisters or best friends. Since I had her so young, she took on the role of being a mother figure to the younger ones more than a few times. I was burning the candle at both ends; sometimes it was good and sometimes bad. I was doing my best with Dawson and the kids, trying to keep up with my real estate job, while trying to take care of myself. In reality, I wasn't doing any of it very well, and sadly, my children were starting to pay the price.

It is hard enough being a teenager in a stable home situation, so it was inevitable that my girls were going to hit a wall at some point with all the instability in their lives. I decided that moving back to Houston, close to family, would be a positive change for us and offer a fresh new start. I also felt that the special education programs had to be better in Houston and thought this would be a good move for Dawson, too.

I drove to Houston one weekend to interview with a couple of modeling agencies and ended up getting a job teaching modeling classes. Real estate was challenging as a single mom, since the schedule was so unpredictable and required weekends. It just wasn't working for me.

I was more than ready to get out of Austin and away from all the bad juju that seemed to follow me wherever I went. I was especially glad to ditch all the bad memories that were, quite literally, around every corner. Almost every day I was afraid I would see Amanda at the grocery store or at Starbucks, and I was so tired of the stress, just waiting for it to happen.

Not to mention, Greg and Elaine had just gotten engaged. It was messing with my head; I hated the idea of Greg ever getting married again. I realize it was completely irrational, because I had remarried once already myself. I was sad to be leaving Hayley in Austin, but by this point she was grown up, on her own, and she needed to live her own life, free from all the family drama that had been with us for years. Most of all, she deserved a break from taking care of me.

By this time, Brenna was fifteen and a junior in high school. She was having a particularly hard time at her school in Austin, and she was bullied relentlessly for reasons I am still not quite sure of. During this time, she was diagnosed with a rare form of arthritis called spondylitis, which required steroids to alleviate the symptoms. A side effect of the steroids was bone death in her hip, which led to avascular necrosis and ultimately a bone transplant. It was a devastating and life-changing diagnosis for her. The surgery was so rare that we had to travel to Duke University in North Carolina to have it performed. She had about six to eight inches of her fibula removed from her leg and inserted into her hip, much like a hip replacement with her own bone instead of hardware.

While the surgery was a success, she had to quit cheerleading and was homeschooled for two months while she recovered.

As if all that wasn't enough, she developed the Epstein-Barr virus, causing her to be constantly ill. She was always fighting some sort of infection. This sweet girl went through so much in that one year and did her very best to keep a smile on her face through it all. She is a true warrior in my eyes.

I believe Brenna became seriously depressed, between the bullying, surgery, isolation at home and being constantly ill. It led her to do the only thing, in her mind, that seemed to ease the pain—physically hurting herself. She started cutting. I asked Brenna to share some of her thoughts about this time in her life so that I could put them down on paper a little better. What she wrote brought me to tears, because some of what she said were things I never knew. Her bravery in sharing this part of her life is a perfect example of the amazing, strong adult she has become. She feels the same as I do, that by sharing our experiences, we might help someone to not feel so alone, and to seek help.

This is what Brenna shared about that dark time in her own life.

> *I would say the cuts I did before the surgery were more to fit in with the people I was hanging around at the time. I did only a few tiny ones and not deep at all. After my surgery and when Robby broke up with me, it got really bad. I felt like I had lost everything and the only thing that made me feel human was hurting myself.*
>
> *I felt very alone. I wasn't in school because of my recovery from surgery, I couldn't go to the bathroom or shower on my own. I couldn't cheer anymore, and the bullying was even worse from home because of texts and Facebook messages I was continuously getting.*

*I also was gaining a ton of weight, and I felt like my high school time was taken from me and ruined. I think Dad was actually considering moving to Arizona or was already living there at this point too. Also after the surgery, seeing how hard it was on my mom to have to deal with me and take me to doctors all the time sucked.*

*I felt like such a burden when everyone else was going through so much. I hated my life, and my mom's was revolving around what I was able to do because she literally had to do everything for me for months.*

*In the beginning, I hurt myself for attention, but it got so bad I was embarrassed to even show or talk about them because I thought people would think I was crazy. But I was in so much physical and emotional pain, burning and cutting was the only way I felt alive.*

*Also, I had gotten really addicted to the pain meds I was on around my junior and senior year in high school. I was taking like three pills every 3–4 hours. It would make me so sick sometimes, but I just wanted to be numb and not care.*

*Now I think about it occasionally and have attempted to a few times, but it actually made me sick to my stomach, since I'm not in the horrible emotional state anymore and I've learned how to handle the need to cut or burn.*

*My school counselor, Mrs. Anderson, was for sure one of my lifesavers and I will never forget how she handled everything I told her. She never once judged me or got upset with or made me feel abnormal. She talked to me like I was a typical teenager, not struggling or hurting.*

*There was also Sophia. Once I noticed that she was declining, I knew I needed to get my shit together. I don't think she knows, but I wanted to be a good influence, and I knew she knew what I was doing, I'm her big sister and should've been a better influence for her when I realized that after I started doing lots of self-talk and self-reflection.*

I know it is hard for people to understand why someone would deliberately hurt themselves or find pleasure in cutting their own skin, leaving lifelong scars. Brenna explained to me that when she cut, she felt an almost euphoric release from her physical and emotional pain. It's as if watching the blood trickle from her skin allowed her to let go of the pain.

Learning that Brenna was doing this to herself because she was hurting so much broke my heart. It also terrified me, because I thought it meant she wanted to kill herself. She told me that it had nothing to do with wanting to end her life. It hurt me so much; here was yet another time when I didn't know how to help my own child. Her school provided a wonderful counselor who helped tremendously. Thankfully, Brenna was slowly able to control the powerful urge to self-harm, but it took years.

I asked Brenna if the divorce from her dad or my own actions contributed to her suffering, and she said it was so much more than just one thing. I still carry tremendous guilt that her life had become so difficult that she felt she had to turn to such drastic measures to feel better. I have learned over the years she was not alone, that many teenagers and adults find relief in cutting. It just was not talked about very much, likely from the shame associated with it.

As a mom, all you want for your children is for them to be happy and healthy, to never feel lost or afraid. You want them to feel that they can come to you with anything bothering them, and you always want to know how to fix things. I had learned with Dawson that no matter how much you love your children and do everything to help them, sometimes it just isn't enough. Now I was learning the same lesson with Brenna.

I honestly believed the move to Houston would help us all to forget the pain that was going on in our lives, but as with so many things, it was just another Band-Aid that would eventually fall off.

CHAPTER 22

W<small>E STAYED A LITTLE MORE</small> than a year in Houston and, as usual, we packed a lot into that year, many highs along with many lows. Staying true to my *love for love* theme, I met Jordan just a few weeks after we moved to Houston. By this time, Greg and I were on good terms and stayed in communication about Dawson and the girls, but also stayed in touch about other things. On special occasions like our wedding anniversary, holidays and birthdays, we would exchange innocent texts with a subtle flirtatious tone, especially after a few drinks. But I was careful to guard my heart and not let it go much deeper than that. I could not go through him breaking my heart again. I stayed focused on the good things in my life, and less than six months later, Jordan and I were engaged.

Jordan was very good to me. He had a wonderful family, great kids, and a career that provided a lavish lifestyle that I admittedly enjoyed right along with him. I had no doubt that I was in love and that we had something special in the making. I was especially fond of his son, Jake, who was the same age as the girls. He was the type of boy any mom would love to have as her own son. He was good looking, played football in high school, and was as sweet as could be; a gentle giant. Brenna and Sophia got along really well with Jake, and I loved the sneak peek at what our future family would look like.

I was thrilled when Jordan proposed in the small, romantic restaurant where we had our first date. But just as it happened with Shane, Greg's face flashed in my mind the moment he slipped the ring on my finger. Once again, I conveniently pushed the confusing feelings deep inside and tried to focus only on the beautiful moment happening right in front of me, as I gave an enthusiastic "Yes!" to Jordan.

This time around I thought being a stepmother would be easier, since Jordan's kids were the same ages as mine and would not need as much hands-on attention as younger children require. Jake lived with Jordan full-time, and his daughter, Maggie, lived with his ex-wife most of the time, so I didn't know her quite as well. There was some trouble in the custody situation with Jordan's children, but I stayed out of it as much as I could.

Jordan was great with my kids, and he was very understanding and patient when it came to Dawson, which I appreciated so much. But as usual, shortly after the engagement, warning signs of impending trouble started to surface. But instead of focusing on what was going wrong in my relationship with Jordan, I started to become keenly aware of a bigger problem brewing. This time, it was Sophia's turn to grab my attention, and boy, was that mission accomplished.

It all began when the girls and I started watching the show *Extreme Weight Loss*, about how people lost dramatic amounts of weight through time, hard work and dieting. At the end of each show, they would have a big reveal to their families, showing off their new look, as everyone cheered and clapped, in awe of the major physical transformation that had taken place. For me, it was a bonding time with the kids, eating popcorn all cozied up on the couch. I never dreamed that such a simple moment in our lives would turn into something so terrifying in the near future.

# Chapter 22

Both of the girls had mentioned they would like to lose a few pounds, so I came up with a fun idea to help them with their goals. They would write down their target weight and put it in an envelope to keep it a secret. After a few months, the person closest to their goal would get a shopping spree to complement their new figure. My well-intentioned incentive was to place control in their own hands, instead of me being the one to point out if they were overeating or not making good food choices. I would later be told, by several therapists and counselors, that was the worst thing I could have done.

Let me just say that Sophia won the weight loss contest, but it was also the start of an eating disorder that spiraled out of control extremely fast. She lost close to eighty pounds in only a few months, just before her sixteenth birthday, and her personality changed as fast as her body. At the same time, I was going through the process of ending my engagement to Jordan. It was not an easy task as he was not taking it well.

The girls wanted to go back to Austin, and they decided to move in with Greg and Elaine while I took care of everything in Houston. Just before things fell apart with Jordan, I had sold my home and moved in with him. Now, I needed to navigate retrieving my furniture and personal items that I had literally just moved the month before, while keeping a safe distance from a very angry ex-fiancé. I was a huge ball of stress and was operating in survival mode. Thankfully, I had not sold my home in Austin, and the people renting it agreed to move out a little early. I was beyond grateful and wanted to get back to my kids as soon as possible.

Once I had settled back in Austin, Sophia's health declined fast as she continued to lose weight. She was pale and her bones showed through her skin, especially in her neck and chest. She was sneaking out of the house, and her behavior became erratic and irrational, with sudden outbursts of rage toward both Greg and me. She was no longer the sweet, goofy girl who always loved being with her family. Once again, I was overcome with the paralyzing fear that I was incapable of helping my own child with something I didn't understand.

We took her to a specialist dealing in eating disorders, and he told us that her life was in jeopardy from the stress her heart was under. My first thought was Karen Carpenter, one of my favorite singers from the '70s who had died from anorexia. There was no way I would let that happen to my daughter. Greg and I were on the same page and decided she needed to go to the treatment center her doctor had recommended in San Diego. We gathered the entire family together at my home and told Sophia what we had planned for her.

"Soph, we love you and we are all worried about you," Greg said calmly as she sat with angry arms crossed.

"We have no choice but to find treatment for you, honey," I added as tears filled my eyes.

We had decided to make a formal plan once we got back from vacation, as we were set to leave the following day. Greg did not think I should take them on vacation during such a challenging time and thought we needed to get Sophia into treatment sooner than later. We actually got into a heated argument over it, but my stubbornness won. I thought it was a good idea to take my girls on a nice vacation to Colorado, with the hope that it might be a game-changer for Sophia to have quality family time, away from Austin. I could not have been more wrong.

She was not happy about the treatment center plans, and she let us know about it as she stormed upstairs, where she disappeared for the rest of the evening. I thought it would be best at the time to leave her alone and give her space to avoid making an already tense situation worse. That was also a big mistake.

The next morning, we got up early and headed to the airport, excited to see my family that was coming in from Houston to meet us in Telluride. Sophia was hardly saying a word to any of us, and I just figured she was still angry about the night before. I let her be and concentrated on trying to have a good time with Hayley and Brenna, who were acting silly and goofing around as usual. As we changed planes in Denver, I could see that Sophia was very groggy and not acting right at all. As we ate lunch at an airport restaurant, she actually laid her head on the table as we ate. She, of course, ate nothing. It was more than just a bad attitude, but she insisted nothing was wrong and that she was just tired. Even though I was extremely annoyed with her, I didn't press for more.

When we finally got to the hotel, she had perked up a bit and was happy to see all of her cousins sitting on the hotel patio, enjoying the crisp cool weather around the fire pit. Just as I had ordered my first much-needed glass of wine, Sophia came over to where I was sitting around the fire.

"Mom, I don't feel very well, something is wrong and I need to go to the room." Her eyes were almost pleading with me, and she looked frightened.

"Okay, sweetie, I'll come up with you," I said, sensing that she did not want to be alone and sort of felt good that she even wanted me around her. The moment we got to the room, the seizures started. I called 911, trying my best to stay calm; but while I was calm on the outside, on the inside I was feeling pure terror.

Watching her have seizure after seizure in the ambulance is a scene no parent should ever have to endure. Her neck would suddenly curl painfully back, and she would be unable to speak for what seemed like minutes. Then her body would relax only for a minute or so until the whole episode started again. I have never seen anything like it, and never want to again.

Sophia kept insisting through her tears and during the moments that she was even able to speak, that she didn't know why she was having these episodes. I was frantic, trying to understand why this horrible thing was happening to her body seemingly out of no where.

"You have to be honest with us, Sophia," the ER doctor asked with urgency. "We can't help you if you don't tell us what happened. Your life is at stake."

Sophia's eyes were filled with terror with each episode, but it still took an hour for her to finally confess to us she had, in fact, taken the pills.

The night before we left for our trip, after we told Sophia about the treatment center, she took a whole bottle of prescription medication. She attempted to take her own life. It was her way of showing us just how much she did not want to go to a treatment center, and her point was made frighteningly clear.

We found out the type of medication after I called a friend in Austin and asked her to go over to my house to look for an empty pill bottle, which she found in Sophia's bathroom. The doctor knew exactly how to counteract the effects of the drug, and the seizures slowly subsided. He explained that this type of overdose does not always have an immediate effect, and it can take twenty-four hours for the body to react. It had been exactly twenty-four hours after she took the pills. The doctor was right.

It was a terrifying journey for me as a mother, and I have never been so afraid and unsure about what to do as I was then. But what I was feeling could not compare to what Sophia must have been going through as a young girl so lost in an eating disorder that had taken over her mind and body.

I was finally able to catch my breath, hearing she would be fine after the medication wore off. Then, just a moment later, I completely came apart at the seams from the hours of stress and not knowing what was happening to my little girl. I was in shock; it hit me at that moment. My daughter wanted to take her own life, and almost succeeded.

After a few days of recovery in Telluride, it was time to head to San Diego without even going home to get her things. It was bigger than just an eating disorder now. We needed to save our daughter's life, and we were doing it blindly, with no script to follow. We hardly knew anything about the treatment center other than photos from the website and reviews ranging from horrible to how the place saved their child's life. Greg was set to meet us at the airport in San Diego, and we would drive her to her temporary home together as a family.

We drove the rental car along the beautifully landscaped road to a one-story home that sat at the top of a hill. It looked like the home of a perfect family, living the good life in California, but it was far from that. It was a one-story mid-century modern brick home that looked as if it belonged in the '70s era. It looked nothing like the treatment center I had imagined. It was a beautiful, sunny California day, but for me, it was one of the darkest days I had experienced since Dawson's diagnosis.

Greg pulled into the circular drive as I sat beside him, paralyzed with fear. Sophia and Brenna sat quietly in the back. Greg and I had been divorced for three years at this point, but that day we were just a family in pain, and nothing from the past mattered. After we had all stopped crying, we silently got out of the car and unloaded Sophia's things from the trunk.

We walked slowly up the steps to the large, brown double doors and rang the bell. It all felt unreal. I can still see those double doors and smell the interior of that house as if it were yesterday. It had shag carpet and a sunken living room with a huge stone fireplace in the middle. There was a large coffee table with an unfinished puzzle that a few sad-looking girls were working on, hardly looking up when we walked in. Even the therapy dog looked sad, but he came up to Sophia, nudging her hand to pet him, knowing it was time for him to go to work comforting the new girl. The place smelled of sadness and despair. I had the immediate urge to grab Sophia, run out the door and never look back. The feeling was almost identical to the one I had when Dawson was diagnosed with autism. The feeling of wanting to simply vanish with your child to a safe place and pretend it was all horrible dream.

Sophia just stood there clutching her childhood black and white polka dot suitcase. Her face was pale, and she had a look of fear combined with exhaustion from the turmoil of the last few days. We were about to leave our broken teenage daughter and her childhood suitcase with complete strangers. We had no idea for how long or when we would see her again. It was one of the most unnatural, helpless and heartbreaking feelings I have ever experienced.

After a brief meeting with the staff, it was time to say our goodbyes. Brenna and Sophia were crying uncontrollably by this point as they hugged for the last time. As I watched them, my heart felt like it was being ripped from my chest and thought I might have a panic attack. The brown double doors closed quietly behind us, and now there were only three of us walking slowly back to the rental car. I fell into Greg's arms and cried harder than I had in a very long time. The terrified look Sophia had on her face as we said goodbye was stamped in my brain. She was alive, and that was all that mattered. But, it still did not calm the relentless fear I felt about leaving her in the hands of total strangers. Was she scared? Angry? She had to feel everything that I was feeling, times a hundred.

Sophia stayed there for three long months, and it was one of the most challenging times emotionally as a mom. Did it help? I think it did, because she is alive and doing extremely well all these years later. But she was also exposed to girls with far more serious issues, ranging from gang rape to molestation by family members, addiction and homelessness with no parental support. She was only sixteen and was dealing with very adult situations, away from her family and was allowed minimal contact with us.

I want to share some of Sophia's own words from this time in her life. It was heartbreaking for me to read about the pain she experienced and how much she needed me. Like most moms, I would have traded places with Sophia any day so that she didn't have to feel afraid. As she and I discussed what part of her story she wanted to share, we both agreed on one thing—we are better people for going through all that we did during that time. Sophia certainly is, and I am in awe of who she is today. Another example of a true warrior.

*I laid in my bed the first night I was there and closed my eyes. I prayed that when I opened them, I would be back in my room at home. The funny thing is I never really prayed before until that first night. I opened and closed my eyes maybe fifty times and when they were closed, I pretended I was back home.*

*I tried so hard to imagine hearing my mom watching Dateline in the other room. I used to hate the sound of a distant TV, but in this moment that was all I wanted to hear. I wanted to walk downstairs, grab a glass of water and sit down next to her.*

*I wanted my mom to come in this terrifyingly dark room and tell me goodnight like she always did. But it was only the nurse that was coming in. She came in every fifteen minutes to make sure we were alive and not doing something I was not supposed to be doing.*

*If I had to go to the bathroom, I had to call out to a nurse to escort me and she stood there watching the entire time, then walk me back to my room.*

*This became my new normal. I woke up at 6am, breakfast was at 7am, snack at 10:30, lunch at 12, another snack at 3:30, dinner at 6pm, and the last snack at 7:30pm. All pre-made meals prepared just for my body type and where I was in my eating disorder. What I needed to survive. Structure instantly became my life with minimal contact with the outside world. I saw things no sixteen year old should ever see and was forced to grow up very quickly.*

*Everything in that place still appears in my dreams. The smells, the sounds, the people almost haunt me. Even though it probably saved me, I don't ever want to go back.*

When it was finally time for Sophia to leave, I had the illusion that when I picked her up, all our problems would be over and life would be better. While she was so happy to see me and excited to come home, our relationship was very strained for a while. I did not expect it and didn't understand why. It was as if she blamed me for all that had happened. I just could not figure out what was wrong, and she wasn't telling me. There was so much tension between us, she ended up going to live with Greg and Elaine full-time, hardly speaking to me for months.

I thought the counselors had somehow put into her head that I was to blame for her eating disorder. They had mentioned more than once what a bad idea the weight loss contest was and that it had ignited the whole thing. It absolutely crushed me that she didn't want to live with me, and nothing I could do or say was right. Even though Sophia never said it, maybe the stability of having two parents living together in the same house, like Greg and Elaine, was the stability she needed. Unfortunately, that was something I could not give her. Then again, maybe it wasn't about me at all, but I sure felt like it. Maybe everything was my fault and I had no clue how to make any of it better.

Not long after returning from San Diego, Sophia started acting out once again. She was sneaking out with random boys and just plain being defiant when it came to following the rules and curfews Greg and I imposed. While our relationship had slowly improved, Sophia only wanted to be at the house of the parent who suited her interests. She was not acting like herself, and out of fear her life was in jeopardy again, we sent her to a different treatment center, this time in East Texas.

This place was more like a boarding school without the school part. It had a Christian-based protocol for getting through to troubled teens and was recommended by a friend who told us it saved their child. It was a ranch with twenty or so cabins surrounding the main building and had the feel of a really nice summer camp for rich kids—and the price tag to go with it.

This place did not accept insurance like the one in San Diego, but we felt it might be a better fit and was really our only option that had a spot available for her at the time. She would live there for nine months, and it ended up being the answer to our prayers. While it was not perfect and it had its fair share of weird things that went on, I believe that the exposure to religion and counselors who treated her like a human being turned her life around.

As I said earlier, organized religion was never part of my own childhood, nor our family's, but I saw firsthand how it can be life-changing for so many. It absolutely opened my own eyes, and while I do not attend church, I do have a private and personal relationship with God. I love the talks we have alone in my car on a regular basis. I believe He was there for me on that overpass, just as He was there for my child exactly when she needed Him.

While Sophia was away at the second treatment center in East Texas, I found myself again leaning on a man for support to help take my mind off how much seemed to be going wrong in my life. On top of that, Dawson had started making these constant yelling noises from the time he woke up until he went to bed. He wore sound-canceling headphones, which was the only thing that made the yells come out softer for some strange reason. He even slept in them.

By the end of the day, my nerves would be on edge from lack of quiet and inability to hardly leave the house on weekends, other than car rides. Thank God Greg and I were able to take turns keeping Dawson, or we would have no doubt gone crazy from the endless yelling and sleep deprivation.

I was barely coming off my broken engagement during this time, when husband number four entered the picture, full of all the sweet talk and support I could ask for.

I knew Steven from our earlier years in Arizona, when I was married to Greg and he was married to a wonderful lady that I was acquainted with. Steven had heard through the grapevine that I was single, and he had just gone through his own divorce. He flew in to Austin on business and got in touch with me, asking if I wanted to get together for dinner. As I said yes, I felt a twinge; something didn't seem right about it, but for some reason I chose to ignore that inner voice once again.

He had the kind of looks that you either thought were sexy or not attractive at all. Sometimes I would look at him and think, *Damn he is hot*, and other times I would think, *He is not my type at all*. The date ended up being nothing special, and I remember feeling a little awkward about the whole thing. But when he took me back to my condo, it was our first kiss that changed everything. Yes, I guess you could say that was some first kiss.

I had not seen or talked to his ex-wife for many years, but it still bothered me, like I was doing something wrong. Looking back, it was just another example of my gut talking to me, and I really should have listened. It felt wrong because it was wrong. Not only did I know, deep inside, he was another Band-Aid on my wounded heart, I was breaking the girl-code by getting involved with a man who was once married to someone I knew and liked very much.

I was in an extremely vulnerable place. I was constantly worried about Sophia, on top of being a single mom with a lot on my plate. Greg and I were not seeing eye to eye when it came to the kids, and there was constant tension between us. I felt Elaine was overstepping as a stepmother at times and voicing her opinions about things that I felt were none of her business. Even if she meant well, I did not appreciate it and was maybe even a little jealous when Sophia and Brenna would sometimes lean on her more than me. I also was jealous that she and Greg seemed to be a happy team; the team that Greg and I used to be. She was living my life, first with my husband and now with my kids. Yes, I know that sounds extremely selfish. I realize that Elaine was actually being a wonderful stepparent, but back then I couldn't see it through the lens of my confused eyes.

Steven took my mind off all the chaos taking over my brain with his constant affirmations of how amazing I was, which at the time was the exact opposite of how I felt about myself. After our first date, he flew back to Michigan, where he was living with his parents. Yes, his parents. We talked for hours on the phone every night for a month. He listened to me dutifully as I talked about all my kids, my fears, my struggles and gave sound advice with heartfelt concern.

Even with all the care and concern he was showing, red flags were boldly waving all around me. Once again, everyone in my life seemed to notice, everyone except me. Hayley kept telling me to slow down and that I didn't really know him as well as I thought I did. My close friends kindly told me their concerns as well, but I just didn't want to hear it.

After a month of long-distance bonding over the phone, I flew to Michigan for a weekend to see him. By the end of that weekend, we were already talking about marriage. I am cringing right there with you. I realize now how insane it was, given all that was going on in my life. How I ever thought this was a great idea, I may never fully understand.

We eloped three months later at a Justice of the Peace a couple of days after New Year, 2013. The only people who knew we were going to do it were both of our parents and his siblings, who we had just spent New Year's Eve with. Oddly enough, my parents seemed totally on board after meeting him once on a visit he made to Austin. They later told me that they had bad vibes about the marriage, but they wanted me happy and thought he made me happy. At the time it was true.

I can only imagine how my children felt when I called them from Michigan the day Steven and I got married. Not my most shining moment as a mother. Sadly, I remember thinking it was my life and I could do whatever I wanted. I thought I was doing what was best in the long run for all of us, and that they would eventually come to love him. I was determined for us to be some sort of normal family, and I thought being married was the way that would happen. I realize now just how irresponsible and irrational all of this was.

That marriage lasted nine months, and we hardly even lived together the entire time we were married. I stayed in Austin with the kids to be able to visit Sophia on parent weekends. I never dug deep into all that was going on in Steven's personal life, I just trusted that the things he told me were true. He had created the illusion that things were all good in his life and that he was part of a new start-up company that was just about to take off. That was the reason he was living with his parents—to save money until that happened.

Did I wonder why a grown man, who used to drive around in a Range Rover and lived in a million-dollar home, was living with his parents? Not really, for some odd reason. I knew his ex-wife's family came from money and that much of their lifestyle was from that, but I did soon wonder why things were so tight financially, there had to have been some savings.

Steven started working for the family business in Michigan for extra cash until the company was supposedly getting underway. Somehow he talked me into buying a little house for him to live in just down the street from his parents so when I came for visits, we had a place to stay. It was a darling little house that looked just like a doll-house in a storybook. It was pale yellow with a huge porch in the back and flower boxes attached all around the railing. I really can't explain why I went along with the plan, especially knowing that I would never live there. It was all presented to me in a very convincing manner, and I willingly jumped right on board with the crazy plan. As I write this, I have to wonder if I believed this perfect little house would some how make my own life seem perfect?

It was during the purchase of the house that the wheels of the relationship started to fall off. I paid for the entire home, I furnished it with extra furniture I had, and paid to have it shipped there. I also paid $10,000 of his credit card debt, which I never saw again. I felt lied to, even though it was my fault for not asking more questions and moving way too fast. I can fall in love quickly, but I can also fall out even quicker. I do believe I was in love at first, and I know he loved me. I'm sure he assumed I was fine, footing the bill for everything, so who would blame him for letting me?

I don't think he ever meant any harm or malice toward me, and he did have many good qualities which I obviously fell for. There was a time when he was a wonderful shoulder to lean on while Sophia was in treatment, and he provided something for me that no one else could at the time. But the whole thing never felt right, and I always felt as if I was constantly making up reasons that it was. I will never forget his favorite line, which was, "I am very resourceful." I think I was the resource in that statement many times. It soon became clear it was time for me to leave a marriage once again.

This was one giant, embarrassing, expensive mistake. Again I have no one to blame but myself. I can only imagine the eye rolling and head shaking that was going on around me. I was humiliated, to say the least, but in a way it woke me up. I really needed to get my shit together, and fast. I realized more than ever that I needed to focus 100 percent on my kids, not on my own emotional needs or the quest to have a normal family . . . whatever that was. Sophia especially needed me more than ever, not some lovesick needy mother who was afraid to be alone. Her time at the treatment center was coming to an end, and I was thrilled to bring her home.

After nine months in East Texas she was a new person. I finally had my child back, but now things between Sophia and Greg were strained. He was much more strict than I was when it came to monitoring the kids. He checked phones and social media accounts, and would call them out when he saw something he didn't like. Sophia did not like how closely she was being watched on social media, and she let her dad know it.

Now, I appreciate that he was harder on the girls than I was, and he was better about making them accountable for their behavior. I continued to be more of a loving friend than a strict parent—not always the right thing to do. Greg and I had a rough year and did not get along while Sophia was away. We constantly fought about what was going on with our very rebellious middle daughters and how to handle it; we were never on the same page. But things did get better between us when Sophia got home and Brenna left for college. It looked like the difficult teen years were finally coming to a much anticipated end.

Sophia had missed her entire junior year of high school. We decided as a family that returning to her old high school in Austin would not be the best choice, as we feared she might slip back into the old crowd. Since Brenna had graduated high school and was in college now, we decided to move to Cypress, Texas, a quiet suburb of Houston. My brothers and their families were still there, and their support was exactly what we needed. I am sure they were convinced that I was officially crazy, but I was excited to be near them again. Greg would keep Dawson in Austin because the special education program was so much better there, while I would concentrate on keeping Sophia on track and healthy.

# Chapter 22

Greg and I would meet in Giddings, a little town between Cypress and Austin two and a half hours apart, to transfer Dawson from one parent to the other. We did it every other week for the next several years, and it worked well for us. Greg had really stepped up to the plate caring for Dawson since the divorce, and I appreciated the small break from Dawson's day-to-day care.

Elaine was great with Dawson, and I learned to let the jealous feelings of Greg and her go. I actually began to really like and appreciate her as a person. Greg and I were getting along much better, and we started exchanging nice texts every now and then. During a Dawson exchange in Giddings one day, I casually asked him how things were going with Elaine.

"It's fine, she is really good with Dawson," he said, in a tone that gave me the feeling things were not fine, and I had to admit I sort of liked it that way. Even though Greg and I had our tough moments, not seeing eye to eye when it came to dealing with teenage daughters and other stressful events with our children over the years, I still missed and loved him. I just didn't let it take over my emotions anymore, a huge step in the right direction. I could see him in person now, and the longing to have him back was easier to deal with. It was a small victory for me, and I started to feel myself get stronger each day and without a man being the one to do it for me.

CHAPTER 23

THE FEW YEARS SOPHIA and I lived in Cypress were the best we had experienced in a very long time. I finally felt that life had calmed down a bit. I was feeling better emotionally and I was more confident in myself. Sophia was thriving, doing well in school and was back to the girl she had once been, making choices every day to stay on track. We laughed together a lot, and the conflict we once had was now gone for good. She also had met a boy her first year back, a boy who would end up changing her life.

Harrison was a bit younger than Sophia, he treated her with love, kindness, respect and patience; something she had not experienced from a boy before. He would soon become like a son to me. Most of all, Harrison helped Sophia to heal from her past, and I credit him for turning her life around.

I reinstated my real estate license and was busy building my business since I did not have Dawson full-time. I was meeting new people and loved being able to see my family, who all lived close by. Best of all, I was getting more sleep than I had in years. I truly believe it was fuel for how happy and strong I was feeling.

Sophia and Greg were finally starting to rebuild their relationship, and naturally I had a new man in my life. Kenny was a successful executive in the insurance industry, and we hit it off immediately. He was tall with sandy-blond hair, gorgeous blue eyes, and a strong, confident personality. I liked how he would take charge in situations, and he was great at planning a fun date night. Shortly after we started dating, however, I broke up with him after a month over a couple of misunderstandings, but it was enough to make me want to move along. I was working hard at not allowing myself to fall for someone that might not be right for me.

A few weeks after the breakup, he called me out of the blue and asked for a second chance. I agreed and things took off once again. We also agreed to take things slow and to enjoy dating with no quick engagements or spontaneous marriages, like we had both done in the past. Another big step in the right direction for me.

Kenny had two wonderful teenage daughters who I adored, he got along well with my girls, and he seemed to care about Dawson. His girls had been through some tough times as children, and I was grateful to be a positive figure in their lives. His youngest daughter, Sabrina, absolutely adored Dawson, which melted my heart. His oldest daughter, Sandy, was the kind of daughter any parent would wish for, and she had her act together more than any teenager I had ever met. Both of them were kind and accepting of my family and me, and I realized I had something pretty special going on.

By this time, Brenna had married her high school sweetheart, Robby, and moved to Savannah, Georgia, after he joined the military. Hayley was loving her life in Austin with her boyfriend, who is now her husband, along with a busy work and social life. Things seemed to be heading in the right direction, and the drama of the last few years was finally becoming a distant memory.

Hayley chose this part in the story to give her point of view on the last several years. Just like it had when I read Brenna and Sophia's words, my heart broke in two. The last thing any mom wants to hear is how much their child was hurt by your actions and how much it had affected her during her college years. But this story is all about real life stuff, even if it was hard for me to accept just how much I screwed up.

*As I entered my freshman year at The University of Texas, life was beyond perfect—I had gotten into the school I had dreamt about attending my whole life, was living in a dorm with girls that immediately became my soul mates and was incredibly happy with who I was and where I was going.*

*A few months into college, I remember getting a call from my mom just before Thanksgiving. My friends and I were getting ready to go to a day party when I picked up the phone to my mom sobbing. Through tears and gasps for breath she told me that my dad had been having an affair with Amanda, her best friend. I immediately hopped in my car and drove the very short, 20 minutes home.*

*My mom and I pored through phone records, and I called the ten consecutive outgoing 512 numbers occurring around midnight from the night he "slept at a friend's house."*

*"Thank you for calling the Four Seasons, how may I assist you today."*

*My stomach flipped and my throat swelled up. I had to hang up right away. Fuck.*

*I dialed the second number.*

*"Good afternoon! Here at the Hilton our customers always come first!" Fuck fuck fuck.*

*This is crazy but in an effort to get information I made up stories about a fictitious piece of jewelry left in a room under the name Swindell, asking the front desks if they had found anything. Most of them wouldn't say but the one that did just so happened to confirm a midnight check in for a Mr. Swindell. The last number on the list was the Holiday Inn Express.*

*The rest of that day/night was a blur filled with wine, tears and dancing drunkenly in the kitchen to mask our pain. That night I changed my mom to get her ready for bed, helped her wash her face and fed her Advil and a sleeping pill. It was the first of many of those nights where I would become the mom and she would become the daughter.*

*I think I held my shit together pretty well during that time, always feeling the need to be the strong one for my mom and siblings. While I was strong in front of my family, I often would explode back at school behind closed doors. Alcohol will do that to you sometimes . . . one minute you are having a blast and the next you are bursting with tears, trying to catch your breath and hardly making any sense to anyone around you. It's incredibly embarrassing looking back . . . always having crying fits about my dad, often turning into tears about my birth father as a cherry on top. I think that's something I've always struggled with . . . appearing to have everything together on the outside, drinking too much and then letting it all erupt. I had a handful of romantic relation-ships throughout college, every single one ending after cool Hayley left the building and drunk, sobbing, Daddy-issue Hayley appeared.*

*My dad's affair was really just the beginning of my family's crazy rollercoaster. My mom was constantly looking to find comfort and love again in other men, immediately falling into serious relationships with wedding bells around every corner.*

*Marriage and divorce became the theme of the decade that followed for my mom. There was a pattern with every man that wanted to marry her—They would ask me to get coffee with them, or if I was lucky they would just call me, to tell me that they were going to propose. I always felt like they were expecting me to scream with joy at the sound of the incredible news. In reality I always died a little inside knowing that it wasn't right and knowing there was nothing I could do about it.*

*My mom was trying to find her way back to the love of her life and was going about it in all wrong ways. All I wanted was for her to be happy and for us to have a somewhat normal life again.*

Dawson was actually doing pretty well, also, and was blessed with amazing teachers in Austin who were committed to helping him be the best he could be. He had learned to communicate a little bit with an iPad for simple requests, like juice and his favorite foods by touching the corresponding picture. His pain was under control for the most part, and he was content both at school and his two homes. He was rarely without his beloved ribbon in one hand and a bowl of Rice Chex in the other. He still could not speak at all, and sleeping through the night was rare; but since I didn't have him full-time, I stopped feeling like a walking zombie. Once again, proof of how incredibly important sleep is for the brain and a sense of well-being.

About eight months into dating Kenny, the familiar marriage talk started to surface, and I was beginning to feel ready for it. A few of my Austin girlfriends had come down to stay with me for a weekend, and after a few bottles of wine, they actually made me sign a handwritten contract. The contract stated that I would solemnly swear to wait at least two years before getting married again. I signed it. Of course in my head I was not making any promises to wait two whole years; that seemed like forever in my world! I did love their sense of humor, even though they were kind of serious about the "love contract" they had drawn up. Another wedding would take place, but it wouldn't be mine.

One afternoon shortly after my friends had gone back to Austin, Sophia was sitting on the sofa playing on her phone while I was in the kitchen making lunch when she suddenly blurted out, "Mom! Dad and Elaine got married!"

I felt like I had just been punched in the gut. I was shocked and I broke into tears. Sophia had just seen a picture that Greg had posted on social media of him and Elaine in an office of the Justice of the Peace.

"Can I see the picture?" I slowly, regretfully asked, as I wiped away my tears.

I wasn't prepared for how much seeing Elaine in her short lace dress and cowboy boots standing next to Greg would hurt me. Even though they had been engaged for years and living together, I never really thought it would happen. In a way, maybe it was good for me that it finally did; seeing them so happy standing together in that photo made it all *too real*. After letting it sink in, I finally felt like I could *really* let go of any hope that one day we would end up back together. He was over me for now, and I needed to accept it. I flipped a switch, I was officially over him. At least I thought I was.

It was not long after Greg's marriage that I would get married for the fifth time. Of all my marriages other than Greg, I felt confident that Kenny was the right choice and would finally be the one who would last the rest of my life. We had waited over a year, and even though a few red flags popped up here and there, I felt they weren't anything to worry about. After all, nobody is perfect, including me. I finally realized that I would never love anyone the way I loved Greg, but that I could still *be* in love, it would just be—a different kind of love.

I also decided it was time to cover up the tattoo on my upper right hip that said "Zeke," Greg's nickname. I know it sounds like a silly mental milestone, but in my mind, covering up his name was like my heart was burying him for good. I also learned that Greg had covered up several tattoos that had my name and felt it was time for me to do the same. I decided to make it into a beautiful butterfly, and as Kenny watched, I winced in pain, but was thrilled that I was finally letting go of the past. I'd had the "Zeke" tattoo for almost twenty years, and covering it up was my final farewell to Greg. Tattoo closure.

SHORTLY BEFORE KENNY AND I married in 2015, I sold my house in Cypress and moved into Kenny's. Sophia had left for college, and I continued to have Dawson part-time. Dawson had adjusted beautifully and enjoyed the long car rides back and forth. Thankfully, the constant yelling that he did had finally stopped for some reason that we will never understand why. This made the entire family happy and relieved. Greg and I were still meeting in Giddings every other week to exchange Dawson, and while I noticed that Elaine rode with him less and less, I didn't think much about it. I liked how Greg acted when he wasn't with her. He was more outgoing and chatty with me, much more at ease for the few minutes we would talk in the Buc-ee's parking lot. Buc-ee's is a Texas landmark. It's a huge gas station, famous for their beef jerky and other Texas snacks, and it became our usual meeting spot. If you are ever on a road trip in South Texas, it is a stop you must make.

My marriage to Kenny started off well, but it did feel a little strange moving into the home where Kenny had lived with his second wife. He did let me make some changes, and I was happy to try and make it feel like my home too. We split the cost of fresh paint and updated the kitchen since that is where I spent most of my time, as the kitchen was my happy place. We kept finances separate, and I took care of all my personal expenses such as my car, clothing, and anything else I wanted, while Kenny took care of the house expenses.

It was a good and necessary arrangement since we both had children we were responsible for, although something about it just didn't feel right. For reasons I can't explain, I felt there was a certain expectation I needed to live up to. Maybe I was putting that expectation on myself with the added responsibilities of two more kids and a husband. My stepdaughters could not have been any sweeter, and my new in-laws could not have been more welcoming. But again, something just was not right, and I could not figure out what.

It wasn't long before that old familiar feeling started to surface. The strong personality that I had loved in the beginning was now slowly becoming something I disliked. He would let me know when he didn't like something I was doing and seemed to challenge any idea I had or decision I had to make, big or small. His idea was always the better idea, and if I didn't agree with it, I was keenly made aware of it.

I kept telling myself the same thing Greg and I would say years ago, "Take the good with the bad."

We were just getting settled into living together. It would take some adjustment and patience to get used to my new life and all that was expected of me. But the tension I felt continued to grow.

The few times I brought up my feelings and concerns, it didn't end well and only left me feeling that I needed to just keep it all to myself, not bring anything up again. I was never physically afraid, but I started to feel uncomfortable in our own home.

I found myself feeling uneasy and anxious at the sound of the garage door opening in the evenings, announcing he was home from work. I knew I should not be feeling that way; after all, he was my husband, and I was in it for life this time. I was going to work hard and get through it. I prayed it was just a phase. The thought of hurting his daughters was something I just didn't want to think about, so I stuffed all my feelings down deep inside and tried my best to ignore my ever-growing unhappiness and uncertainty.

In May of 2016, I bought a small condo in Austin. I reasoned that it would help with the trips back and forth for Dawson, and I could stay there for long weekends with him instead of bringing him home to Cypress. I found myself really looking forward to those trips to Austin. I found comfort with my girlfriends, as well as time alone with Dawson. I felt like I could breathe there, and my little condo became my hideaway. I knew I could not do it forever, but for the time being, the routine was working for me.

I never told anyone how I was feeling about my marriage to Kenny, not even my dear friends. But my parents started to sense something was very wrong and could see I was not myself. I was spending more and more time at their house when I was home in Cypress, to avoid time at mine. I finally erupted and told them everything I had been holding in. It felt so good to finally tell them as they listened with kind ears and gave me loving words of encouragement, just as they have my entire life, never judging harshly and always wanting whatever made me happy. Yes, my parents truly are the most amazing humans on the planet. Little did I know, I was soon going to learn that my rocky marriage wasn't the only thing I would need to deal with, not even close.

2016 WAS ALSO FILLED WITH excitement. Greg and I became grandparents for the first time when our grandson, Wyatt, was born. We all traveled to Savannah, Georgia, where Brenna and Robby lived, to be there when she went into labor. It was just the original Swindell family, we were all together without our spouses for the first time since both Greg and I had remarried. Elaine had stayed home with Dawson, so it was just the five of us, and oddly, it felt like no time had passed. Hayley had named us The OG Squad, for the original gangsters. All the girls were in good places in their lives, and the past drama had dissipated. It was such an exciting time for us, and everyone was happy to be together as a real family again. At least sort of a real family.

Did I feel anything for Greg at that time? Maybe a little, but I didn't get that feeling in return, so I did my best to brush it off and just enjoy the time waiting for our new grandson to be born. We ate dinners together and went bowling, hoping that Brenna hurling a bowling ball down the alley over and over again would jump-start her labor. We did have one false-alarm trip to the hospital, and we all laughed harder than we had in a long time, being silly and taking home videos of us dancing in Brenna's hospital room. We drove through Taco Bell in the middle of the night after the false alarm and devoured several six packs of beef tacos, just like old times. It felt good to be with my own people where I could be myself—maybe a little too good.

Wyatt decided to take his sweet time coming into the world. The girls needed to fly back home for school and work, but Greg and I stayed. It was so amazing to be there together during that incredible moment. I will never forget Greg and me standing beside our daughter's bed as she lovingly held her new son for the first time; our first grandson. I was completely overwhelmed with love. Love for Brenna at how natural it was for her as she held and nursed her baby, love at seeing the perfect little face of this new little life who was my grandson, and a new kind of love for Greg. I remember thinking it seemed like only yesterday when Greg and I were in our own hospital room when Brenna came into our lives. We were so in love back then, and seeing our baby have a baby ignited something inside me that I can't even begin to explain.

Later that night after leaving the hospital, we had dinner together at the hotel bar, just the two of us. Soon we would both be going home to our own separate lives, and I felt a twinge of sadness that our time in Savannah was over. We chatted easily, laughing about all the events that had happened over the week. We were clearly having a good time together.

Our observant server asked, "Where are you folks visiting from?" assuming we were a couple.

We giggled and said, "Oh, we are not together. We used to be married, but not anymore. We just had our first grandbaby!"

"Well you sure get along well! You don't see exes having dinner and laughing together very often," she said with a warm and approving smile.

As we finished dinner, and with a little help of liquid courage, I asked, "So, are you happy being married again?"

I was shocked when he finally said with his head down, "It will never feel like it was with you."

I always knew that Greg still cared about me, but this was the first time he actually said it to me in person, face to face, not in a late-night text or an obligatory birthday message. He said it to me sitting right beside him, and it felt so good to hear it almost scared me. My heart melted.

"I feel like Elaine has been taking money from me. She makes up crazy stories about the missing funds when I bring it up," he continued as he looked up at me. "Lots of weird money things that just don't make sense."

I felt like he wanted to tell me more, but I didn't press it.

"She is so great with Dawson, I . . ." Right then, he cut himself off from saying anything more. He looked defeated, like the effort required to just say the sentence had exhausted him. We decided it was probably time to get the check and call it a night after a long but wonderful day. We left our suddenly serious conversation at the table.

It was so strange: The man I had lived with, cared for, had children with, loved for so long, was going to his own room, especially after all that had happened that week.

"Do you want to come have one more drink in my room?" I could not believe that sentence had actually come out of my mouth, and by the look on Greg's face, he was a little taken aback as well.

"I think I will just head on back to my room, but thanks," he quickly said, as my face flushed with embarrassment.

"I am so sorry, I didn't mean it in that way. Too much wine, and that probably came out wrong," I lied. I wanted him to come back to my room because I didn't want to say goodbye. Sex wasn't my motivating factor, and to this day, Greg doesn't believe me when I say that it wasn't. In my mind, I already knew how good our sex life was; it was more about just being with him. I missed just being with him more than anything else. I felt like I could completely be myself with Greg. I missed being his teammate, and now we were going to miss being grandparents together. We were going to share that role with our new spouses, and it all felt very strange.

We gave each other a hug that lingered a bit too long as the elevator doors closed, and we said goodnight. We went our separate ways to our separate rooms and back to our separate lives. I was already dreading going back home, and I could feel that maybe he was thinking the same thing.

It was time to get back to reality. I decided that night in my hotel room that I would forget about our dinner and focus on the joy of being a new grandmother. I also decided that I was going to work harder at my marriage. Maybe I just needed to change my way of thinking and not be afraid to speak up, even if it meant a fight. I knew that continuing to hold my feelings in was not doing anyone any good. I wondered if Kenny even felt anything was wrong? I knew he had fought constantly with his second wife. Was this normal for him? I glanced at the hotel room clock, and seeing it was 2:30 a.m. reminded me that I had a long day of travel only a few hours away.

I popped a Unisom to turn my brain off and fell asleep thinking about Brenna and Robby with their new precious baby. I thought about my daughter who was now a mother and how incredibly proud I was. I thought about how much I hated leaving her, knowing all the emotions that come with being a new mommy. Then I thought about Dawson, and how much I wanted to see him after being gone so long. I missed him desperately and longed for one of his special sniffs, the one he does when he's missed you. It's his way of giving a big hug. It was time to go home.

Dawson had not been himself lately, and I was starting to worry.

CHAPTER 26

Shortly before the trip to Savannah, we started to notice that Dawson was losing weight. He had been on the "fluffy" side for years, so at first we thought it was a good thing that he had started to thin out. He was getting taller as well, so we thought maybe that was the reason he looked thinner. But we also noticed that his ankles were starting to turn in, and he seemed to be losing the little muscle tone he had. But what started to really worry me was how his energy level had decreased.

Dawson had always enjoyed taking long walks around the neighborhood, but those walks were progressively getting shorter and shorter. After three or four minutes, he would turn around, take my hand and lead me back home. Then he would lay on the couch, exhausted from the short walk. He was also biting himself on his hands and pinching his body, leaving tiny bruises up and down his legs. To me, it seemed as if he was in and out of pain, but I couldn't pinpoint where the pain was coming from. The main challenge of having a child who is nonverbal is trying to figure out where the pain is coming from or why he is upset: a constant guessing game that rarely has a clear answer.

We had always assumed his pain was from the bowel disease and his need to poop. Poop is another thing that has always been front and center in our world. When he poops he is happy, when he doesn't he is not. His poop schedule was our barometer when it came to his happiness. He had started taking Humira injections, and it seemed to help with inflammation. Now he was in a different kind of distress, and it was my mission to find out why.

One day Dawson was lying on his tummy at his favorite spot in the house on the entryway rug. It was just inside the front door, and he loved looking at the tiny rainbows that would form on the floor from the sunlight shining through the cut-glass door. He was starting to get "twisty," which is something he does when he isn't feeling well or is in pain. He can twist and contort his body in ways that are cringe-worthy because he is so flexible, or if you are familiar with medical terms, hypotonic.

He will sometimes make loud groaning noises as he is twisting. This is a cross between a cry and a roar and usually without any tears. When he is twisty, there is not much you can do for him and it will usually pass within a few minutes, sort of like a bad stomach cramp would. He does not want you to comfort him or hug him, which is difficult as a mom and goes against all motherly instincts.

I walked over to him to rub his back in an attempt to calm him and noticed that his right shoulder blade was sticking up higher than the left as he was lying facedown on the floor. At first, I thought he might be doing it on purpose as he sometimes does when he gets mad. It's as if he is purposely trying to pop them in and out of the socket. But when he calmed down it still was sticking out. I hadn't noticed it before, and I notice *everything* when it comes to Dawson and his body. I think all moms are mini doctors and know their children better than anyone, noticing even the tiniest changes physically and emotionally. Even with my girls, I can figure out what is wrong with them usually before we even get to the doctor, or tell something is wrong simply by the slightest change in their voices. "Mommy powers," as they would call it.

When Dawson stood up, I took his shirt off and gave him a once-over. Even standing up, his shoulder blade continued to stick out, and I also noticed his lower stomach area looked like it was caving in a little on one side. It looked like it might be scoliosis, but I knew how rare that was in boys, especially showing up at such a late age.

Dr. Google went straight to work, and after about thirty minutes my heart started pounding with fear. Scoliosis alone isn't really that big of a deal, but when it's combined with other symptoms, like the ones Dawson was having, it is a whole different ballgame. Everything I found kept taking me to pages that had to do with neuromuscular disease. The same feeling of panic I had when I googled *autism* so many years ago started to set in.

I called Greg immediately and asked him if they had noticed anything with Dawson's back. I knew he thought I was just overreacting and over-googling. In his usual calm demeanor, he told me to stop worrying, that it was probably nothing. Naturally, I didn't listen and that Monday I called the physical medicine doctor Dawson had seen for his weak ankles, and we set up an appointment for an x-ray of his back.

The x-ray confirmed that it was, in fact, scoliosis. He already had a 38-degree curve, and it was too late for any kind of bracing. Our next step was to see his neurologist for a full evaluation to see if it would get worse and to find out what was causing this sudden curvature in his spine. In my gut, I already knew. So many signs of neuromuscular disease were there: the weakness, fatigue, muscle wasting, and now scoliosis. How could this be happening to this child who was already battling so much? There was no way God would allow this to happen to an innocent boy who had already been given more than his fair share of obstacles to overcome. I wanted to be wrong—please let it be something that at least had a cure or some sort of action plan we could follow. There was no way he could have two medically incurable problems. That would be way too cruel!

I went to the neurologist by myself with Dawson. Greg still didn't believe it was anything to be too concerned about and reassured me that it was probably nothing. I admit, I sometimes fall into the hypochondriac category, but the problem is, I'm usually right. While I would sometimes diagnose myself with some kind of terminal brain tumor after a bad headache, when it came to my kids, I was usually spot-on.

After an hour with the neurologist, he agreed that something was wrong. The sudden curvature of Dawson's spine was very suspicious and consistent with neuromuscular disease. He ordered lab work for genetic testing, and we would need to see a slew of more doctors while we waited for results. Now I was officially terrified. I had no idea there were so many different types of the disease, along with several other diseases that present similarly. Another search for the needle in a haystack. Sadly, I knew this process all too well.

But this time I was wiser and more experienced. I knew that I needed to educate myself as much as possible in order to ask each doctor the proper questions. I had learned over the years that you have one shot to ask questions when you're face to face with a specialist. Otherwise, you play an endless and frustrating game of phone tag with nurses instead of the doctor. I made appointments with all of Dawson's doctors in Austin first, since they had most of his records. I was so grateful to have my little condo so I didn't have to drive back and forth. At first, Kenny was very supportive and loving during this difficult time. I was visibly upset a lot. I was so wrapped up in Dawson that I didn't even think about anything else, and Kenny did his very best to show he cared.

I dove into my research, learning the terminology relating to different things it could be and the causes. I eliminated certain diseases first, then focused my energies on narrowing down the ones I felt could be possible so that I could ask questions about those and not waste my precious office time. I was constantly on my computer at home, and I am sure I was not the same smiling, attentive new wife and stepmother I had previously been. The only thing I cared about was what was happening to my son. I felt completely alone in my pain and overwhelmed with pressure to act *normal* for everyone else.

I could tell Kenny was losing interest in hearing about it, especially as it dragged on. As I spoke, I could see his eyes drift off, replaced with a look of boredom. Looking back, I'm not sure that I blame him. Dawson wasn't his own flesh and blood. I cared deeply about his children, they were great kids, but didn't feel the same *love* I feel for my own children, the love that I would hurl myself in front of a bus for. I constantly struggled with these feelings, and I really felt like something was wrong with me. Do all blended families have the same problem, or was it just me? I felt too guilty about these feelings to share them with anyone.

Balancing being a stepmother to Kenny's kids and a mother to my own was difficult, especially when I was so consumed with Dawson. Maybe it was my own fault for putting so much pressure on myself to be there for everyone, treat everyone with equal amounts of love, all while pretending it was a piece of cake. I think it's harder to establish a bond once a child is set in their ways as a teenager. They are used to the way of life they enjoyed before the stepparent ever came along. The same goes for expecting stepchildren to be thrilled and accepting of a new stepparent. There is nothing easy or natural about any of that.

Stepparenting is not as easy as the *Brady Bunch* made it look, and I really admire families who succeed. I can't even imagine how difficult it would have been if I had stepchildren who hated me. Mine could not have been any better, yet it still was a difficult adjustment to navigate through.

I think when stepparents are introduced when the kids are younger, the bond is easier to form, easier than in the teenage years.

I experienced that firsthand with Greg and Hayley. If it's ever mentioned that Hayley is not Greg's daughter, he becomes very upset and rightfully so, as Greg raised her. Never once in our marriage, or even after our divorce, did he ever act like she wasn't his child. Greg's own family treats Hayley like a full-blooded Swindell. Greg happily went to every daddy/daughter event, school activity, and endless dance recitals. He tucked her in at night, read her bedtime stories, bought her her first car, paid for four years of college and a big wedding, because Hayley is Greg's daughter, and because that is what daddies do. She has been in his life since she was three years old, and that bond was easily formed. Truthfully, it was not always roses between Greg and our girls, especially during the divorce; but his love for all his girls, biological or not, was always there, even if he sometimes had trouble expressing it.

During my marriage to Kenny, I found myself closing down more and more. I was stuffing all the sadness and fear I was feeling because I didn't want to burden anyone with it. I cried a lot when I was alone, in the car, in the shower. Sometimes I would cry just watching Dawson struggle with the smallest things. He had stopped swimming and jumping on the trampoline, he preferred sitting for most of the day. He was getting thinner and thinner, and he looked so tired with dark circles under his eyes. Even running errands with him became a challenge because he would become exhausted after an hour and would want to just sit down. I even ordered a wheelchair for him. I was convinced he would be wheelchair-bound in a short time, but from what, I still had no idea.

Our next appointment was with a specialist in Austin who specialized in neuromuscular disorders, and this time Greg joined us. I had taken Dawson to see an orthopedist for his spine a few weeks earlier, and he felt the curvature was, in fact, due to a yet-unknown neuromuscular disease. He cautioned me that sometimes a true diagnosis never occurs, due to limitations in genetic testing. The orthopedist wanted to wait and see if the curve got worse before we talked surgery and wanted another specialist to take a look at him before making any more decisions.

I arrived at the neuromuscular doctor's office before Greg and was a nervous wreck. I sat there, chewing on my nails in the small, sparsely furnished waiting room. It brought back all the memories of fifteen years ago, along with all the familiar feelings of uncertainty and undeniable fear. What were we going to hear, or not hear, from the doctor? As soon as Greg walked in, I was able to breathe again. Just having him in the same room made me feel stronger. Even though we were not married anymore, we were in it together. I stood up and walked over to give him the hug I so desperately needed. This was our baby—everything in our past melted away as we sat side by side in the cold, impersonal waiting room.

When we were called back to the exam room, my heart was pounding through my chest, even though I had done the same thing countless times before. Even Greg had a concerned look on his face. It was rare that he got worked up or showed concern, and he was far from an over-reactor.

Dawson chose to sit on the floor as usual. He exchanged the ribbon he carried for a purple rubber glove he immediately noticed in a box on the counter, motioning to us that he wanted it. Just then, two doctors walked in the room. They were all business, and very little small talk was exchanged. One was a medical student, and he was the one who started the initial questions with his clipboard in hand.

They asked Dawson to stand up from the floor. In doing my research, I knew what they were looking for. It's called the Gowers' sign and indicates weakness of the proximal muscles, usually in the lower limbs. This is exhibited by pushing on the legs when rising. I already knew Dawson was doing that.

"I do see that he is positive for Gowers', but it's not too bad at this point," the doctor said. Naturally, all I heard was "at this point," and my brain immediately went to Defcon 5.

The main doctor examined him from head to toe for about forty-five minutes while continually asking questions. When he was done, he pulled up his little chair on wheels and began to speak.

Once again, my ears began to ring, just like during Dawson's autism diagnosis. I had a hard time understanding what the doctor was saying as I battled holding back my tears. He was certain Dawson had something more than just autism. His words confirmed that we were dealing with something more serious. He ordered more tests and more specialists. Just like in 2001, it was happening to us all over again. Our sweet boy was blindsided by another undeserving blow, and it hit me just as hard as it did the first time.

I was an emotional mess by the time we made it to the elevator. When the three of us got to the parking lot I fell into Greg's arms, and he held me as I cried uncontrollably for what seemed like forever. I never wanted him to let me go, and all I knew was that I did not want to drive back to Cypress; back to the home where I was so unhappy and felt that no one understood my pain. Only Greg truly understood me. As we both held each other, both of us felt the same heartbreak, sadness and uncertainty for all that was ahead. The only thing I wanted to do was to stay right there with him and cry for our son who had just been handed another life sentence.

A COUPLE OF MONTHS WENT BY and Dawson's spine continued to get worse. This meant that whatever was wrong was, in fact, progressive, and surgery would most definitely be in his near future. He was at about a 50 percent curvature, and we were getting conflicting opinions from his various doctors about when he should have the surgery. One doctor thought we should wait a little longer, while the other thought we should have done it long ago.

The surgery was not going to be easy for him by any stretch. The fact that he was so severely autistic with an unknown neuromuscular disease made it even riskier, which only left me feeling more scared and confused about what to do. Trying to get several doctors on the same page was an almost impossible task, especially when we didn't really know just exactly what we were dealing with.

Some of his genetic testing lab work had come back and, of course, it came back with no definitive answers. He had genes of "unknown variance," which basically means something was off, but there was not enough information to point to a specific disease. More tests were ordered, followed by more specialists who were not able to give us good information or provide a game plan on how to help him. My heart was breaking for Dawson, as he had no way of understanding why he was being put through so much. I wasn't sleeping from all the worrying and the what-ifs. How bad was this going to get? How quickly would this progress? How long would he be able to walk? Was this something that would eventually take his life?

Around that same time I became friends with Jenn. She was a beautiful blonde, an avid tennis player, and a loving, devoted mom to a son the same age as Dawson. A mutual friend of ours had introduced us at a neighborhood Happy Hour, and we clicked immediately. Our boys had both been diagnosed with autism at a young age and had very similar characteristics, except that Jenn's son suffered from severe seizures, and he had some language. He had also suddenly started deteriorating physically with no medical explanation. They were going through test after test, many of the same tests that we were doing, seeing every doctor they could and, like us, never getting any real answers. Having a friend like this is very special. No matter how kind your typical friends and family are, or how much they listen to you cry, someone who *truly* gets it is an incredible gift. Watching your child suffer through life elicits emotions only someone going through the same thing can really understand. Jenn got me and I got her, and we quickly formed a bond that I will always cherish.

Jenn's son deteriorated quickly and, sadly, within a year after we became friends, he passed. I watched this amazingly beautiful family go through the worst nightmare of their lives, with more grace and courage than one could ever imagine. He passed with no real answers as to why his body failed so quickly and no name for what it was. I felt like her son and Dawson had started a marathon together, and out of nowhere, with no warning, her son sprinted right past him. I almost felt guilty telling her Dawson was sort of leveling off, not getting too much worse. I also could not help but feel that the very same thing could happen to us at any moment.

All that was happening also made me think of my beautiful niece, Justine, who passed away from cancer recently. She was so young, in her early twenties, and I sadly watched my sister go through the same gut-wrenching experience with her sweet daughter. I have been through a lot in my life, but I can't think of anything more horrible than watching your own child pass. Witnessing my sister's heart literally breaking right in front of my eyes is something I will never forget. I had a sickening feeling that I might be getting a glimpse into my own future. I had now witnessed three people close to me lose a child. Sometimes I felt like the reason I was watching these families go through such tragedy was meant to be practice for when my own heart would experience the same grief. I don't think I could ever be as strong as Karie, my sister, or Jenn. Seeing their faces go through the worst pain imaginable is something I will never forget. I know I will look back and draw strength from them, if that time comes.

I tried so hard not to let my brain think about Dawson suffering any more than he already had. As horrible as it sounds, I prayed that if that time did come, it would be as quick and painless as possible. I could not bear the thought of him being in pain and not having the language to tell me how to help him and what he needed to feel better. It was, and still is, an indescribable feeling of helplessness, and by far the hardest part of having a nonverbal child.

I became so wrapped up in trying to figure out what was happening with Dawson that I started to care less and less about my situation at home. I hung out at my parents' house more because I felt I could really talk to them about my fears, and they always had loving arms to comfort me. I slowly stopped talking about my feelings to Kenny because all it did was lead to a fight, and I certainly did not have the energy for that anymore. I hated that I felt stuck in yet another relationship that I knew wasn't working. I knew I should be trying harder to make it better, but just didn't know how. I also didn't understand why I really didn't want to.

As much as I tried, it was hard for me to smile and live each day pretending all was good when inside all I cared about, or had the energy for, was my own family and helping Dawson. I felt horrible for Kenny's girls, as they deserved a much better stepmother than me, and I knew it. My little Austin home became the only place where I felt like I was okay and could just be myself, free from my own expectations and judgments. The holidays were coming, and I knew it was going to be challenging in a million different ways. I love the Holidays, but this year I was dreading them.

Christmas 2016 came and went and we were still not making much progress with Dawson, but thankfully he wasn't getting worse. His spine was still curving, but his energy level was consistent. We decided to go with the doctor's opinion of waiting a bit longer before doing the surgery.

That Christmas was difficult for me in so many ways, especially having to entertain like everything was completely normal. In the midst of it all, we hosted Kenny's huge company Christmas party at our house. The past years had been fun, as I loved being the hostess; but this year I did not feel like celebrating anything and just wanted to get it all over with.

Brenna and the baby flew into town after the New Year in 2017, and I was so happy to have them home, a welcome distraction from all that was going on in my head. Greg was in Houston at that time and had decided to make the short drive to Cypress to see our girls and, most of all, Wyatt. Elaine had also driven in to see them as well.

Looking back, it was extremely generous of Kenny to allow Greg and Elaine to come over and hang out. It must have been a bit awkward for Kenny, but he never showed it. Kenny did have some wonderful qualities, and there were moments when I felt if I could just focus on those, all would be fine. Allowing his wife's ex-husband to come hang out at his house while he was at work could not have been easy and was definitely a kind gesture I'm sure most men would not be thrilled about.

We all sat around the living room laughing and playing on the floor with Wyatt. Greg's mom even came by and stayed for a while and was so happy she was able to meet her great-grandson. I was surprised when Greg decided to stay after his mom and Elaine left late that afternoon, knowing Kenny would be arriving home soon. When he did get home, they shook hands and chatted as if nothing was strange about this very strange situation. We ordered pizza and played games around the patio table, including Kenny and one of his daughters. It was a pretty special day, even if it was a little unconventional, with all of us hanging out like we were one big happy family.

By this time, I was really good at ignoring my feelings for Greg whenever we were around each other. I had accepted that we would never be anything more than just the parents to our children, and I had to be okay with that. I was so happy everyone was getting along, laughing together and enjoying each other for the kids' sake and now for our grandchild. The two men in my life were sitting at opposite sides of the patio table, while my heart was still softly aching for the one it shouldn't be. My heart was also wondering why Greg stayed so long that night, and why he didn't leave when his mom and Elaine had left earlier that afternoon.

I knew things were not perfect in Greg's relationship with Elaine by the little things he shared with me over the years, including that night in the bar in Savannah; but I believed he was committed to her and I admired that. She was so good with Dawson, despite her financial issues. I assumed Greg simply overlooked her money thing because she showed such love for Dawson and cared so much about his well-being.

She did so much for Dawson that was good, and I think we all appreciated that, including me. In the end, did it make the other things she did okay? I'm sure there are many different thoughts and opinions on that. We all make mistakes and to me, it's admitting those mistakes, learning from them, as well as taking responsibility for them. If that does not happen, nothing can truly be resolved or forgotten. But all that was none of my business at that time, and I stayed out of it.

A few weeks after our time together in Cypress, I was in Austin with Dawson. Having some unexpected free time, I texted Greg to see if he happened to have a leaf blower I could use. The spring leaves blanketed my driveway to the point I couldn't even see the concrete.

About an hour later he texted back and told me to come outside. I walked outside to find him unloading a brand-new leaf blower from the back of his truck. I almost didn't know what to say, I was so surprised at his kind gesture.

"Thank you! You really didn't have to do that," I said, with a big smile.

"No problem," he said, smiling back at me as he climbed in his truck and drove down my driveway, the leaves blowing in his wake.

I walked back in the house thinking that something felt really different during that moment in the driveway. I knew Greg better than anyone in the world, and I knew there was more behind the simple gift of a leaf blower. He is a man of few words, but his actions have always spoken volumes, in good ways and in bad. If you are in Greg's heart, it is the best feeling in the world. If you're not, or you wrong him, he will kick you out and never look back. I had felt kicked out for so many years—was I now back in?

He was softer than I had seen him in a while, and he looked at me differently. I started putting small things together: the time he programmed all the radio channels in my new car after I told him I didn't know how to do it, and he was definitely texting me more than usual.

# Chapter 27

Nothing scandalous or wrong, just short texts about little things, like a new XM channel he knew I would like, or something funny he saw on TV. On top of that, we were communicating more with everything that had been going on with Dawson. But it didn't really hit me until he showed up with a simple leaf blower.

CHAPTER 28

G REG'S BEHAVIOR WAS confusing me. Together with all that was going on with Dawson and the stress constantly simmering at home in Cypress, it was a recipe for many sleepless nights. I felt like a strange storm was brewing in the ocean of my brain, and nothing would calm it. Kenny and I had a trip to Mexico planned, and I was really going to try and focus on him, try to relax and have some fun. Maybe this trip was exactly what we needed to get back on track.

The trip ended up being a complete mess, and I was crying before we even checked into the hotel. I don't remember the specifics, but I do remember thinking our situation was hopeless and it was never going to get better. How in the world did I get to this place *again*? His kids would be torn apart if I ever left, and I could not even begin to think about how Kenny would react if I decided to leave. I didn't think I could deal with the embarrassment and shame again, not only for me, but for my kids too.

I had grown to love Kenny's family and once again had involved my kids in these relationships as well. I hated to put any of them in another awkward place because of my choices. None of it was their fault. Would my issues become their problem once again?

I told myself that leaving was not an option, and maybe counseling would help. I was going to try and make the best of it. I would learn to just keep my feelings to myself and focus on all the good stuff in my life. Who had a perfect life or perfect marriage, anyway? It certainly could be worse. Kenny had some great qualities, we had a beautiful home, plenty of money, and everyone other than Dawson was happy and healthy. There were times when we got along great and seemed to be on the right track, but it felt forced, and I was walking on eggshells more often than not.

Maybe it was all in my own head. I just needed to get my own shit together and stop being so selfish. The last thing I needed in my life was *another* divorce. Thank goodness I had the peacefulness of my condo in Austin whenever I needed it, and I was so grateful to have the respite and the chance to regroup. It could work, I simply needed to change my attitude. After all, my attitude was the only thing I had any control over in a life that was suddenly out of my control once again.

I continued pouring most of my energy into researching Dawson's still unnamed illness. I became as educated as I possibly could on various types of neuromuscular disease. He had so many symptoms, but nothing pointed to one specific disease, which made me start to doubt it was even that at all.

He was scheduled to have a muscle biopsy in Austin, and even though it would be hard on him, I hoped at least it might give us some clarity. He had MRIs done of his brain, and nothing new had shown up since the previous one. We also did some more blood work that had not come back yet. I was hopeful that between the muscle biopsy and the blood work, maybe we would finally figure out what kind of monster we were dealing with. I needed answers to calm the chaos that was going on in my head, and I needed them fast. I could slowly feel the toll that it was taking on me. I was keeping things bottled in so tight that I was afraid I would explode like a shaken can of soda at any moment.

I drove to Austin the day before we were to meet with the surgeon for the muscle biopsy at Dell Children's Hospital. It would not be a long surgery, but they would have to put Dawson under because of his autism and lack of understanding of what was happening. Greg and I met with the surgeon, who was actually a friend of ours, and everything about the meeting was smooth and familiar.

"Dr. J," I always called him. He was soft spoken, kind, and put our minds instantly at ease. Greg and I laughed and joked around in the waiting room just like old times. One thing for sure, Greg and I have always had the same sense of humor and find comedy in the smallest things most people would never get or think is funny.

As we waited for Dawson, I had mentioned to Greg that I wasn't very happy at home, and I told him there must be something seriously wrong with me that I couldn't seem to make a marriage work.

"Don't be so hard on yourself, you were great at our marriage. I was the one who fucked up, not you." Hearing him say it made my heart flip. It was something I had always wanted to hear from him in person. I literally felt like my soul had suddenly been healed by that one simple statement.

I had worked so hard through the years to get over Greg. Now, sitting in that waiting room, I was mad at myself for letting those old familiar feelings creep back into my heart. It was scary, and even though it felt good, I didn't want those feelings back. I needed to work on my marriage to Kenny and put all craziness out of my head. The more I fought, the harder it became.

Something had switched that day of Dawson's surgery between Greg and me. A familiar energy had surfaced, and it made me feel alive again. Maybe all the difficulties with Dawson had made us closer as friends, and it was nothing more than that. There was no way he could be feeling the same thing I was feeling, and I decided once again to guard my heart and stop thinking about it. Nothing good would come out of it, even if he was starting to have feelings for me again. I was NOT going to commit adultery of any kind, and it already felt like cheating just thinking about it. If I've learned anything from the past, it's that even thinking about cheating does not usually end well.

We found ourselves alone in the doctors' waiting rooms a few more times in January 2017, with the same damn familiar feelings sitting right between us. I felt so much comfort from Greg during those doctor visits, and it was eerily reminiscent of when Dawson was a baby going through the autism diagnosis. Except this time we were older, wiser and had already been to hell and back.

There was a softness in our new relationship that had not been there for years, as if the past had been stripped clean of all its ugliness and pain. When we were together, it felt like wearing the warmest, most comfy sweater in the world, after thinking it had been lost forever. Having Greg beside me when dealing with Dawson's illness was the kind of love and support I craved. But I knew that it was too late for us, and we had to live in the now. I needed to just be happy with the good place we were in and focus on what was happening with our son. Nothing else needed to matter.

After another long day of doctor appointments, I was cooking dinner at home in Cypress, listening to '90s Country Music on Pandora. That station always took me back to a time when life was so magical and full of promise. It took me back to the good times with Greg—not a good idea when my marriage was on the brink. It made me happy in a nostalgic sort of way and was an escape from the present. If I could not be with him physically, I still had the memories.

I was making tater-tot casserole and remember so clearly the text that came over my phone as I poured the hamburger meat over the tater tots. Yes, that is how clear it was.

# Chapter 28

"I really miss you," appeared on the screen.

My heart actually leapt in my chest and tears welled up in my eyes. We had said stuff like this over the years, but this time it felt different. Fear, excitement, sadness, elation—all at once. This was all wrong in too many ways to count. But what I was feeling was so familiar and clear, I almost didn't know how to deal with it. It was the same love I felt almost twenty-five years ago when I married Greg, and suddenly, there was nothing wrong about it. Except for one very important fact—we both were married to other people. My husband was about to come home from work at any minute, and my stepdaughter was upstairs, waiting to eat dinner with us.

I decided to text back. "I miss you too, Zeke."

I had not called him by his nickname in years, but now it felt more natural than ever.

"Maybe someday when we are old and gray, we will be back together," I texted back with shaking hands. I had always thought that maybe, just maybe, Greg and I would end up together, but it would be in a retirement community when we were in our 80s. I could see the scene so clearly in my mind. We would be playing the same board games we loved to play when we were young and madly in love, sipping our Pinot Grigio with ice from our oversized wine glasses, on the front porch of our tiny patio home. It was crystal clear.

Bubbles were on my screen for a few minutes while he was typing something back to me. It was long, whatever it was, and I took a giant gulp of my wine and held my breath as I waited.

NOTHING PHYSICAL HAD HAPPENED between us since the divorce, but I almost felt like it had by the way my whole body reacted to what I read in the text. I was in trouble and I knew it. He said he still loved me, always had, and he didn't want to wait until we were old and gray in a retirement home to be together. He said he wanted me back sooner than later. *Sooner* than later? All of a sudden, everything that was so wrong in my life, that had ever been wrong, felt so incredibly and overwhelmingly *right*.

I wish I would have kept what he had written, but sadly I deleted it. I knew I should not have been having that kind of conversation with my ex-husband and was terrified Kenny would find out. None of it was fair to him by any stretch. I was so confused about what I had read that it made my head spin, and I could hardly continue making dinner. For a moment, I felt that I was no better than Amanda, and she was the last person I wanted in my head right now, and the last person I ever wanted to be associated with. But was I? What was this? Was it better that it was my ex-husband and father of my children, or worse?

"Now what?" I said out loud, as I put my phone down and quickly got myself together. Maybe he had been drinking and had no idea what he was saying. It had happened before, and if that was the case, I would most likely get an apology the next day for overstepping, and nothing more would be said. Yes, that was it. He would text me tomorrow, say he was sorry, that the vodka had gotten to his head, and all would be back to "normal," whatever that was. And to be honest, I would be fine with that.

As excited as I had been hearing that Greg still loved me, the panic of how we could ever make it work overwhelmed me. It seemed truly impossible, too many lives would be turned upside down, and it made me anxious just thinking about it. I shoved everything I had read in the last fifteen minutes deep inside, hoping it would stay there for good.

I served dinner, cleaned up the kitchen, did a load of laundry, watched TV and went to bed with Kenny just like any other night. But *everything* felt different now, and I had no idea how to handle what my heart was feeling. It was sheer terror, while at the same time, the most calming feeling of love that I had felt in a very long time.

I tossed and turned the entire night with all the inner conversations I was having. Was I actually even considering ending my marriage, hurting the children, the families, the judgment and embarrassment . . . and get back with Greg? There was no way it would work. We had way too much garbage from the past, and it would be just another catastrophic ordeal for our own children when it would inevitably blow up in our faces. I could not put my children through any more madness as a result of my own poor choices.

I told myself over and over that I needed to make my marriage work and stop living in the past. Yes, what Greg and I once had was beautiful and real, and it needed to stay in the past where it belonged. I was not even sure if our girls would want us back together again after everything that had happened, as they had grown to love and care about our spouses. I knew my brothers and their wives already thought I was crazy and were tired of all my poor decisions. I was an embarrassment to them, and another divorce would not help.

Before I finally fell asleep, I decided that just knowing Greg had always loved me was going to have to be enough. The whole thing felt crazy because it **WAS** crazy! I woke up the next morning feeling like it had all been just an insane dream, and I had a pounding headache from way too much wine. I reached over to get my phone from the nightstand, clicked the screen and saw there was a message from Greg.

CHAPTER 30

Greg's text was not an apology for overstepping, and he had not been drunk the night before. He still meant everything he had said, and yes, still loved me and wanted us to be together. While I had convinced myself in the middle of the night that I didn't want any part of it, the feeling had now dramatically changed—it was *all* I wanted.

I would be seeing Greg the following Monday in Giddings to drop Dawson off, and we decided to talk in person then. I thought that maybe by then he would have had a change of heart, and we would get back to the lives we were living. Maybe I was still guarded because I had been so hurt in the past and wanted to prepare myself for that possibility, but this time felt completely different for reasons I still can't explain.

The best for all involved would be for Greg to change his mind, even if I really didn't want him to. It was completely selfish for me to want this so badly; I knew how much it would hurt people. It was all extremely confusing, and I desperately needed advice from someone I could trust with this *new crazy,* and that someone was my parents.

I got to my parents' home, poured a glass of wine, and told them I really needed to talk to them about something and wanted their honest opinion. The moment I told them what Greg had said, my mom started to cry. Was she mad at me? Was she afraid to tell me I was crazy? It was neither; they were tears of joy! My parents had always loved Greg, even after all that had happened, and they knew how special our love had always been.

Greg had been so good to my parents while we were married, and they thought of him like he was their own son. They knew I had not been happy, they had seen it all over my face for months. Actually, they had seen it for years. Both my parents said they had not seen my face light up more than when I told them what was happening. As always, they gave me their full support and encouraged me to disregard what others would think. "You two have always had something magical. You only have this one life and your happiness matters, not making sure everyone one else is happy." It was actually the first time anyone had ever said that to me out loud.

As someone who has always cared what people thought of me, I knew it would be the mother of all judgments. I hated the thought of hurting people, and there was no doubt people would be hurt, especially the children. For the rest of the weekend, I could hardly eat in anticipation of seeing Greg and wondering how our talk would go. What was he thinking? What would happen? Would he change his mind again?

I hated the feeling that I was being sneaky and deceitful in my own home, but on the other hand, I had a spring in my step that had been missing for a long time. I could hardly look anyone in the eye, I thought they could see everything going on inside my head.

"How do people actually have affairs?" I thought, over and over. I wasn't even doing anything, and it was already eating me alive with panic and guilt.

Monday finally arrived, and I was filled with emotions ranging from excitement and love, to fear and confusion. I loaded Dawson in the car, handed him his bowl of Chex and a ribbon, and we were on our way to meet up with Greg. One of the bonuses of having a nonverbal child is that you can tell them all your deep dark secrets, and they won't tell a soul. Dawson is a vault of knowledge and will go down in history as the world's best listener!

I told Dawson that we were going to see Dad and that we were going to have an early lunch at Whataburger, just the three of us. I told him that Daddy and I were thinking about getting back together, but that it was all very complicated. I asked him to tell me if he had any bright ideas or thoughts about all of it. He said nothing, so with a giggle I took his silence as an excited "YES! I would LOVE THAT!" Thank you, Dawsie!

When we arrived, Greg was already there, parked in his truck in front of Whataburger. One would have thought we were on a first date, the way my heart felt. I had seen and hung out with Greg plenty of times over the years during kid events, doctor's appointments, and Dawson exchanges, but never felt anything close to what was happening. He even looked at me in a different way: no longer as the scorned ex-wife, but as if he had not seen me in years. It was the look of pure love, and it made my heart flip once again.

It was like no time had passed as we slipped into a booth in the back of the restaurant. We were just Dawson's mom and dad who loved each other very much. Greg and I sat side by side. We hadn't sat so close to each other in nine years, and our legs were pressed together under the table. Dawson sat across the table from us with a funny look on his face, and we both burst out laughing as we guessed out loud all the things that he must be thinking.

After a few minutes, Greg took my hand and held it as we talked, gently stroking my fingers—nothing ever felt more natural. He had not changed his mind over the weekend as I had secretly hoped/not hoped. I asked him how he thought we were actually going to do it. After about an hour of talking through scenarios and details of what was ahead, Dawson started getting antsy. Greg needed to get back to

Austin and take him to school for the rest of the afternoon. We were both sad that it was time to part ways.

We left with the plan that we would wait until the summer to break the news, so that at least Kenny's daughter would be off to college and maybe it would be easier for her. We would all be empty-nesters except for Dawson by then, and less lives would be affected. We talked about what our children would think and knew they would feel blindsided. We knew we would have to be patient with everyone's reactions and understand that everyone would think we were absolutely crazy—and I agree, it was crazy! It was not going to be an easy task, but by the end of that one hour in the Giddings, Texas, Whataburger, we knew it was what we both wanted without a shadow of a doubt. Several more long lunches in our Whataburger booth with Dawson made everything even more crystal-clear. We decided the shit storm that we would inevitably go through would all be worth it in the end, as long as we were together.

Four months felt like an excruciatingly long time to wait, but in reality, it would be just a blip in the big picture. My main worry was how to act like a normal wife at home when I would be living a lie. The thought tore me up during every car ride back. I wasn't sure that I could get through it. I thought about calling Greg and telling him the whole thing was off, that it was insane and wrong on so many levels. But the thought of not taking the chance to be with Greg felt even more wrong than staying in a bad marriage just for everyone else's sake.

One minute I felt like a giddy teenager in love, and the next I felt like the worst person in the world. I was the person I hated most, a liar and a cheater, at least I felt like a liar and a cheater. I did not want to go home to my house. It wasn't even my house, it was his house before we got married and had never felt like my house. I realized just how much I felt like a visitor in my own home—it had never felt right. Kenny and I had actually started the process of buying a new home before the whole thing happened. I had thought it might help all the feelings that I didn't quite understand about my marriage. I should have known from experience that a new house does not solve anything.

I knew that a house had nothing to do with our problems; it was much more than just a house, we were not right for each other. I needed to tell Kenny that we need to postpone the house we planned on buying, but what would be my reason? He would most certainly ask that question, and it was an argument I dreaded having.

I wanted to turn the car around and go back to Austin to *my* house and hide away until May.

Needless to say, we couldn't keep it a secret until May. A few weeks after reading the text while making tater-tot casserole on an evening in February, we decided to tell our family the news. We couldn't put it off any longer. Some took it well and, understandably, some not so well. Brenna cried, but hers were not tears of joy, as we had secretly hoped. She was worried about our spouses. It was the first thing she mentioned through her tears. It broke my heart to hear her so upset, knowing Greg and I were the sole cause.

My brothers and their wives listened as I told them our plan over the phone, but I could hear the doubt in their voices. I knew they were all weary with my spontaneous choices in the past. Some of Greg's family had concerns, and we were made aware of those as well. We knew it would happen and needed to be understanding. Not everyone was going to jump aboard our crazy love boat. We both understood and respected how much they cared for those that would be affected. We created the mess and would have to deal with the negative thoughts.

Sophia's reaction was a whole different story, and it still brings tears to my eyes when I think about the day we told her. Greg and I surprised her at her college. She had no idea we were together that day and thought she was only meeting Greg for lunch at a local Mexican food place. Since the Texas Longhorns baseball team was playing Sam Houston State where Sophia attended college, Greg was planning to see Sophia before the game. I decided at the last minute that I would make the one-hour drive as well, but she had no idea I was coming.

When she walked in, she was shocked to see Greg and me sitting on the same side of the booth, and a little closer together than what divorced parents normally do.

When she walked towards us with questioning and very concerned eyes, she asked, "Is there something wrong with Dawson? Why are you here too, Mom?"

"Everything is fine, sweetie, we just need to talk to you about something," I calmly said.

Greg took over as he put his arm around me. "I love your mom so much, Soph. We have been talking and we want to get back together, and we want to do it soon."

Sophia started crying, and her tears were no doubt tears of joy. "Are you serious?" she asked as she wiped her eyes.

"We have never been more serious about anything. How do you feel about it?" Greg asked.

"It's like a dream coming true! When is it going to happen?" she asked with a burst of excitement through her tears.

We ordered a a few margaritas and explained our plan the best we could, without knowing exactly what it looked like ourselves. Only that we were going to try and wait a few months, until summer. It meant the world to us to have Sophia's support with our crazy plan, and seeing her so happy made it even better. Needless to say, she missed her classes the rest of the day.

I had told Hayley a few days before everyone else over the phone. While she was undoubtedly shocked, she was supportive and happy for us; if she wasn't, she was kind not to say so. She also naturally had the gut instinct to protect me and was a bit worried I might get hurt again. She did not want to see me go through what I had worked so hard to overcome. I completely understood her fears, and I'm sure she was going through waves of emotions as well. She had worried about me for years, something a daughter should never have to do in the first place. I know she was also preparing for yet another bomb to be dropped for all the world to see, and of course all of that had to be on her mind.

Obviously we couldn't wait until the summer to tell our spouses, since the cat was out of the bag. Now that we had told our families and children the plan, there was no turning back. I was firm in my beliefs that I did not want to end up having an affair with Greg, but with our newly professed love, it was bound to happen if we didn't act fast. There was no way I could do that to Kenny and his girls, nor did I want to hurt Elaine by being any more secretive than we already were. It was already taking a toll on me mentally.

To this day, telling our spouses was one of the hardest things I have ever done. We both cared about them, otherwise we would have never married them. But those relationships were far from perfect, and we hoped that would ease the shock. It still did not make it any easier to hurt someone, most of all Kenny's children. They deserved so much better than me, and it killed me knowing how much this was going to upset them. I know it was shocking and incredibly painful for everyone, as I had been there myself many years ago. Maybe that is why it was so hard for me, I could honestly *feel* and understand their pain better than anyone.

I am not sure what is worse; having your heart broken, or being the heartbreaker. When you are dumped, at least you get surrounded by love and support, and people feel sorry for all that you are going through, as they should. When you are the dumper, the world hates you and thinks you're cold and calculating. I even felt that way myself for a while. I hated how I'd hurt the families who I'd grown to care about, who had welcomed my children and me into their lives. For that,

I will always carry tremendous guilt. Nobody deserves to feel the pain of sudden heartbreak and rejection. Being the one to pull the trigger felt just as horrible.

It was also difficult walking around knowing, or at least feeling, that the world was judging me without knowing the full story, our own families included. I don't think I ate for days with the whirlwind of emotions—from joy that Greg and I were going to be together, to sadness for how many people were hurting because of us.

After the dust from the bomb we had dropped settled, it was just Greg and me alone in my condo in Austin. It felt like we were hiding away in a bunker until it was safe to come out. The guilt and anguish was still ever-present, but being with the true love of my life made it all bearable. Nothing in the world had ever felt so right in a situation that was so wrong for others. We were finally alone after we put Dawson to sleep. Alone for the first time in almost nine years, and all that bottled-up love was finally free to come out.

Greg and I knew every inch of each other's bodies, but it almost felt like the very first time when we finally got back to the bedroom. Feeling his skin, and exploring what we once thought had been lost to us forever, was intoxicating, to say the least. I had missed everything about him for so long, it almost didn't seem real as we were tangled up in bed, never wanting to let go. We both were filled with so much raw emotion, the love between us engulfed the room as if time had never passed.

That first time didn't last long, and we still laugh about how quickly Greg lost control in the best kind of way. The sounds that came out of his mouth made us both roll with laughter after I sarcastically asked with a shy grin, "So did you . . . ?" We were back, sense of humor and all.

After our laughter subsided and tears of gratitude filled our eyes once again, he softly said, "I'm home."

WE were home. We held each other without saying a single word, soaking in all the love and never wanting to let go. Almost afraid to let go for fear it was all a dream. Nothing could have been more beautifully real.

It took sixty days for both of our divorces to be final. Sixty-one days later, on May 12, 2017, we flew to Scottsdale, Arizona, where there is no waiting period required to get married. We said our vows for the second time to each other on the patio of the Embassy Suites Hotel under the scorching Arizona sun as sweat and tears streaked our faces. It was just the two of us and the hotel front desk girl who stood as our witness, while total strangers vacationing around the pool curiously looked on.

Almost twenty-five years earlier we eloped, young kids in love who barely knew one another. This time we knew everything about each other and had a lifetime of memories standing right beside us. Those memories silently cheered us on and held us together like a warm, loving embrace, assuring us that we would be fine. All the memories of love, pain, fear, gratitude, and most of all, forgiveness, gave us permission to be right there in that magical moment.

All in that same week, Greg closed on the house that he'd sold before it even hit the market, both our divorces were final, we flew to Arizona to get married, and we closed on the new house we'd bought together. I still don't know how we pulled the whole thing off. I smile when I think about the faces of the gals around the closing table as we told them our confusing love story while signing all the documents for our new home.

"This needs to be a book!" The closing agent exclaimed as she clapped her hands with excitement.

"Trust me, I have been wanting to write a book for years," I sheepishly said. "I have had my title for so long, but my ending was never clear."

Now, my ending was perfectly clear. I chose the title, long before I had even written one word. I truly believe the heart knows things before we are made aware of them. Would I have changed any of the events that led to this point in my life? That is a tough question. All the pain, humiliation and anger of the past have shaped the magical relationship that Greg and I have today. Without that, I'm not sure where we would be.

We now have a sense of peace every single day as we raise our special little boy together and spend time with our adult daughters, and now two grandchildren. Greg fills me with an indescribable feeling of being loved that no one else has ever been able to duplicate. He expresses it in ways that only I know of and in ways only I understand.

I am no longer consumed by fear about what lies ahead for Dawson, or any other obstacle for that matter, because I know Greg and I will get through it together. I believe autism initially tore us apart, but it was another heartbreaking diagnosis of his that brought us back together. Dawson, in a way, saved us. He certainly saved me and brought me back home, right where I have always meant to be.

# Epilogue
## 2019

I CAN'T BEGIN TO PUT INTO WORDS how much being able to share my story has profoundly impacted me. While the events I have written about were difficult to relive at times, I also discovered just how incredibly blessed I am. I have seen firsthand the beauty that can come from forgiveness and the power that love can have on a family that had once been so shattered. My hope for you, as a reader, is that maybe you don't feel alone in your own pain or confusion, and that my story gives you hope that you can get through anything.

People have been through far worse things than my family, as many of our struggles were self-inflicted. I realize more than ever how amazingly, and sometimes painfully, beautiful my life has been, and I am grateful for all of it. There is no way we would all be where we are at this moment without these experiences, and we are closer than we have ever been as a family. Even at our very worst, we had so many times of love and laughter that was alway present, even when I didn't always realize it.

Greg and I have been re-married for over two years now and celebrated our twenty-sixth (sort of) anniversary on March 21, 2019.

Yes, we celebrate two anniversaries every year, because each of them means something very special to us.

Recently, friends and family have been asking me how things are going now that we are back together. I can sense a slight hesitation when they ask, they are probably waiting for me to say, "Well, that was a bad idea!" or "What was I thinking?" The truth is, everything IS fantastic and could not be better! When people ask me how things are going, I find myself trying too hard to explain how happy I am, for fear I might sound like I am faking my happiness, like I did so many times in the past.

Another friend asked me recently, "How did you guys get through everything from the past, and how can you trust again?" For me, there is not one answer to that question, and it's likely different for other couples who have worked through similar situations. Are there other couples like us out there? We need to have dinner and compare notes!

I thought I would share what has worked for us, what statistically never should have. Even now, we will stop and smile at how we did it. We marvel at how we were able to come back from so much pain and hurt as if time never passed, to be better than we ever were. This is what worked for us, and these same simple actions can work for any relationship.

From our hearts, we both apologized for our mistakes. We both made them. We talked at great length in that booth at Whataburger, and we both chose forgiveness, both in giving it and receiving it. Is it that simple? It sure can be, if you both desire it!

We **DO NOT** bring up the past if we can avoid it. The past is the past, and absolutely nothing good will be gained by bringing up things we can do nothing about or change. This was a tough one for me, especially after a few glasses of wine and a very active mind!

**TIME**! Yes, time does heal all wounds and can mend a broken heart. While things will never be forgotten, we don't let them define who we are now. We are both very different people after ten years apart, but our hearts remain the same, and our hearts were always meant for each other and our family. It just took time, lots of time, to realize that we needed to do something about it.

We hold hands whenever possible, say and do nice things for each other, and do not put ourselves in positions that could possibly hurt the other. No more staying out late with the girls, and cell phones are no longer secret-keepers. We communicate when there is something that needs to be addressed instead of going silent. We are more understanding of each other's differences now and no longer sweat the small stuff. It really is that easy, and a simple recipe for a successful marriage that simply took a long time for us to figure out.

I have wondered how many couples end up getting remarried after a divorce. I would guess 90 percent want nothing to do with their ex-spouses, just from asking around. But I am always happy to hear when people tell me about their own parents or people they know getting back together. It shows me how strong true love can really be and all that it can endure.

When it comes to all of my marriages, I often explain that I was not trying to catch up to Elizabeth Taylor. I've jokingly said that countless times and will probably say it many more. It's a *fun fact* that I have been married six times—five if you don't count the one I married twice. It depends on the day and if I am in a playful mood, which is usually the case, how I will respond when asked about my colorful love life. I find it easier to laugh and joke about myself rather than explain how or why I have said "I do" six times, all before the age of forty-nine. It may sound like I am proud of it, or that I don't take it seriously, but that is far from the truth. I will carry this scarlet letter around with me forever. I did it, and I have no one to blame but myself.

To be honest, I am embarrassed. I can't hide it, lie about it, or pretend it never happened. It's public record and is brought to light every time my credit is pulled. "Are all these people you?" My go-to response is to say I am in the witness protection program and have to change my name a lot. Much easier and less embarrassing than the truth as to why so many different last names pop up.

There is no question people were hurt, most of all my own children and the children of the men I married. I was unintentionally selfish, thinking I was doing the right thing each and every time. Those children were amazing, and I cared about them all deeply. I hope they all know that they deserved better than what I could give them as their stepmother, and that it was only out of my own weakness that I felt overwhelmed much of the time. Maybe I was overwhelmed because my own children were still young or because Dawson was in a particularly difficult phase. I was barely hanging on, trying to raise my own.

I know it may sound like a lame excuse, but with all of my heart and all that I am, I went into each relationship thinking, "THIS is the one! I love him, and he is perfect for me and my children. We will all be one, happily blended family. Easy peasy!"

The truth is, I don't think I was ever capable of loving anyone else the way I should have, and obviously the relationships did not have a strong enough foundation to endure the challenges. While I probably deserve to be cursed at, made fun of and judged harshly, I wasn't the only one to blame for things falling apart. In the words of Rob Base & DJ EZ Rock, "It takes two to make a thing go right." The same applies for when things go wrong.

I never went into a marriage thinking, "Oh my gosh, it will be SO FUN to get divorced in a few months! I love losing thousands of dollars, being an embarrassment to my family and hurting children, this will be AWESOME!" Getting divorced sucks. One would think that after each divorce I would have reevaluated, been more careful, more selective, moved slower. I can't answer why I didn't, despite pleas from my children, family and friends. Each time I felt like I knew exactly what I was doing, but I realize now I was desperately trying to fill the giant hole in my broken heart.

There were plenty of family members who would try to get me to *think clearly* and *take things slower*, but I just would not listen. I think sometimes that I was attractive to men because I had money and could take care of myself financially. Unfortunately, more than once, that turned into me taking care of their financial troubles, which only came to light after the ink had dried.

I have always been terrible with arguments and confrontation, so when those situations would arise, I had no idea how to handle them. In all the years that Greg and I have been married, we've hardly fought, about anything, so it was something I had minimal experience with. Greg has never been condescending, and he's never said mean things to me, even in the worst of times. My father and my brothers are just as kind, considerate and respectful. I had never personally experienced a man with a quick temper, a condescending tone or a mean side.

Of course, there were wonderful times with all of my ex-husbands, and yes, most still live in Texas. I was filled with hope and love in the beginning, or I would never have married them. I will always look back with a smile on the good times, the laughter, the experiences, and I will be forever grateful. They all had incredibly kind families who opened their arms to me and my kids. I very much regret any pain they endured as a result of my mistakes.

I have wanted to write my story for so long. The one thing holding me back was fear of what people would think, and that I hadn't figured out the proper ending. I thought my story would be about finding true love again with someone *else*, and the ending would be *that* love story. Even though I dreamed of Greg and me getting back together many times over the years, I never really thought it would happen. I even had my title, "Rounding Home," picked out, years before I wrote a single page. I thought how cute the title would be if we ever did get back together . . . That dream became the most beautiful reality. Now it's time for the good stuff!!

My girls are all doing fantastic. They are following their passions in life and are in strong, loving, and committed relationships. Hayley and Brenna are now married to wonderful men. Sophia is engaged to be married in December of 2020 to Harrison, her high school sweetheart who I adore beyond words. I believe that everything that happened in their childhood shaped them to be resilient in so many areas.

Brenna and Robby have two children now and we are loving being grandparents. Best of all, they moved back to Texas and live just a few minutes from us. Brenna is in beauty school and set to graduate in early 2020, after spending four years as a brave military wife. In her free time, which is not much these days, she does photography on the side, and is very talented. She is an incredible mama. It's amazing to watch my once very strong-willed child, who went through so much as a teenager, blossom into a strong woman and mother in all the right ways. Her husband, Robby, proudly served our country in the Army and is now taking college classes, preparing for his next career and life after the military.

Hayley and Sam were married in the fall of 2018. She has always been our little entrepreneur and is always involved with various endeavors. Hayley is, quite honestly, the rock of the family and one of the most courageous and strong women I know. She never gave up on her dreams, while always being a wonderful big sister to her siblings and, most of all, a wonderful daughter. The only way to describe her is that she is "pure sunshine." Her husband, Sam, is the son of Dr. Wakefield, who I spoke about in the book. How about that fun twist of fate? Best of all, just as I was wrapping up this book, I was informed that they are expecting their first baby! We are so proud and honored that our family is now part of the Wakefield legacy.

Sophia is about to graduate college with honors, and she plans on becoming a special education teacher. She has also started her own successful videography business, filming weddings on the weekends. Most of all, Sophia is healthy and the happiest I have ever seen her. Thinking back to the time when she tried to take her own life seems unreal now. She makes the choice every day to get better mentally and physically, and I thank God every day that she does. She is the daughter who goes above and beyond, making sure everyone feels important and loved, another ray of sunshine in our lives! She is the one who tells me every single day how much she loves and appreciates me, and she would literally do anything for her brother Dawson. I have to thank her fiancé, Harrison, for the gift of being such a supportive and encouraging figure in her life. These two will no doubt take on the world as husband and wife!

To say how much I love my girls is an impossible task. They have all endured so much in their lives and have all grown into amazing young women, when they had every excuse not to be. They put up with so much when I was not of *sound mind and body* for so long, and never once did they make me feel bad about it. While they all faced challenges as teenagers, we all survived, and we all learned valuable lessons, every muddy step of the way. Would I ever go back to those years? Oh, heck no! I think I am still exhaling from the stress of it all. But, I am beyond proud of the women they are today. They are the kind of daughters any mother would be blessed to have. I thank God, that mother is me.

Now let's talk about Dawson. This precious young man turned eighteen years old on February 4th, 2019, and has changed so many lives in so many ways. He still has his good and bad days, and there are still times when he is sad or in pain and we have no idea what is wrong or how to help him. He had his spinal fusion in the summer of 2018 and grew three more inches once his spine was straightened out. He went into surgery 6'0" and came out nine hours later 6'3".

We still do not have solid answers about his mysterious neuro-muscular disease, but whatever it is, it is progressing very slowly, and he is walking just fine. I am happy to say the wheelchair I bought a few years ago is collecting dust in our garage. He still cannot speak at all, but he speaks volumes with his sweet smile and expressive eyes. He has been to hell and back, most recently surviving sepsis shortly after his spine surgery that could have easily killed him. He is a true fighter, and while we have no idea what his future looks like, his whole family will be fighting right beside him.

Being an autism mom will always have its tough days. There are times when I look at him with intense sadness for the life he should have had. The life that, I believe, was taken from him, due to a simple round of vaccines he should have waited to receive when he was healthier. While I think his neuromuscular disease is a product of bad genetic luck, I believe his autism and brain damage are from me not listening to my motherly intuition.

People will argue this fact with me for the rest of my life, and that is okay. I respect other people's thoughts on the subject, just as I would like my thoughts to be respected. There is a safe way to vaccinate, and it's not a one-size-fits-all protocol, as we are programmed to believe. We saw it happen right before our eyes, and Dawson pays the price every single day.

I know there isn't such thing as Stage 4 autism, but that is what I call it when I try and describe Dawson's situation. When I say Dawson has Stage 4 autism, it helps whoever I am talking to, understand just how profoundly autistic he is.

It is no fault of the person I am speaking with when they say things like "Does he play a musical instrument really well?" or "I bet he is really good at math!" And my favorite: "Does he know all the baseball stats?" I will laugh and say he can't do any of those things, but hot damn, he can out-whistle anyone!

People also often tell me how their brother, uncle or nephew has autism and do amazing things, like participate in sports, play in the band, or even attend college with some help. I am so happy when I hear success stories about people living with autism. It shows how early diagnosis, therapy, a supportive school, and a loving family can make a significant impact on a child's future that once may have seemed bleak. Those people have what I call Stage 1 or 2 autism. Yes, they still have challenges in their everyday lives and may always need help with specific tasks that seem easy to others. They can go on to form lasting friendships, hold down a job, and even get married someday. But that will never be true for Dawson because he has Stage 4 autism.

He will need lifelong care and will never live on his own. He can't speak, so someone will always have to be his voice and make sure he is never mistreated. He needs help with bathing, brushing his teeth, shaving his face and getting dressed every single day. He doesn't know how to blow his nose, make his own food, or even wipe after using the restroom. Someone will always have to do those things for him for the rest of his life, because that is what living with Stage 4 autism is like.

Sometimes it feels like we are swimming in a giant ocean with only a tiny life raft to get us through the storms that constantly come and go in Dawson's life. We are thankful when the waters are calm, but we are prepared for the next storm looming just around the corner.

We have no idea what is ahead for him physically, or what we will do once he has to leave high school at twenty-one. The storms are brewing and will eventually hit us. Our tiny life raft has managed to keep us afloat, even when I felt as if I could not hang on for one more minute. But for now, the waters of Stage 4 autism are calm, and I will continue to hold on tight for Dawson as long as it takes, and wherever it takes us.

Dawson has profoundly changed me as a human being, and his autism has brought me to the brink many times. But his autism has also taught me more about love and patience than anything else ever could. Dawson's autism may have been a contributing factor to the downfall of my marriage to Greg, but it was also the contributing factor to us getting back together. Dawson will always be my hero, just by getting up and living each day—with a voice that has been silenced and a body that continues to test him. He does it with a smile on his face and always with a ribbon in his hand to comfort him. This boy is my whole heart.

Last but not least, there is Greg, aka Zeke, the love of my life. By now everyone knows just how insanely in love I am with that man; I wrote an entire book about it. I can't imagine my life without him, and the fact that we got a second chance is something I will never, ever take for granted. He is my forever love, my best friend, and the person I will grow old with. He fills me with contentment and provides me with an indescribable feeling of peace. We are living our lives together once again, and we will continue to care for our special boy together, until we no longer can. We get to be grandparents together and watch our daughters navigate through their own amazing and sometimes bumpy world together. Together is where we were always meant to be.

While we no longer have millions of dollars, the big fancy house, or the glamorous lifestyle we once had, I could not be happier. We are no longer expected to pick up the tab, bail people out of a financial crisis, or make huge donations. I find pure joy in movie night or a *Dateline Mystery* marathon at home with a bowl of popcorn and a box wine for dinner with Greg by my side. I love coffee or Happy Hour with girlfriends and, most of all, simple family gatherings with our kids and grandkids. All this, well within our budget.

I look back and feel truly blessed at the life I have lived so far, even with all the painful moments that were sprinkled in. Naturally, there are things we all would like to do over; but without the hard times, the good times would not feel so special. While I look back with a smile on the glamorous early years, I am beyond grateful for my beautifully regular life now, including my complicated past, and

## Epilogue

I would not trade it for the world. I am human and far from perfect, and that is more than okay—something I never would have said years ago. Most of all, I feel joy once again and am no longer consumed by fear of the unknown. I have truly rounded home, and I am right where I was always meant to be.

# About the Author

Sᴀʀᴀʜ Sᴡɪɴᴅᴇʟʟ ʟɪᴠᴇs ɪɴ ᴛʜᴇ Austin area with her husband, Greg, a former Major League Baseball player and 2019 Texas Sports Hall of Fame Inductee. Sarah is a commercial actress/model and has been working in the industry for over thirty years. She enjoys spending her free time with her four grown children and several grandchildren who reside in Texas as well. Sarah is an avid moviegoer, loves yoga, true-crime podcasts, and advocates for children and adults with autism and other disabilities. Her son was diagnosed with severe autism at the age of eighteen months and continues to touch peoples' hearts to this day.

Made in the USA
Coppell, TX
07 November 2019

11069145R00150